SCHOOL ENVIRONMENT
in
NIGERIA
and the
PHILIPPINES

Edited by:
Prof. Akpanim N. Ekpe
Dr. Imelda L. An
Dr. Jake M. Laguador
Dr. Ngozika A. Oleforo

authorHOUSE®

AuthorHouse™
1663 Liberty Drive
Bloomington, IN 47403
www.authorhouse.com
Phone: 1 (800) 839-8640

Published by AuthorHouse   02/11/2015

ISBN: 978-1-4969-6670-4 (sc)
ISBN: 978-1-4969-6830-2 (e)

Print information available on the last page.

Any people depicted in stock imagery provided by Thinkstock are models, and such images are being used for illustrative purposes only. Certain stock imagery © Thinkstock.

This book is printed on acid-free paper.

ABOUT THE EDITORS

Professor Akpanim N.Ekpe is currently the Dean of Social and Management Sciences, Akwa Ibom State University, Akwa Ibom State, Nigeria. He is a research fellow of Institute of Public Administration of University of Liberia, fellow, National Association of Research Development, Editorial Board Member, Institute of Local Government and Public Administration of Nigeria. He has published widely in reputable journals in Nigeria and the overseas.

Dr. Imelda L. An is currently the Dean of the College of Education, Arts and Sciences at the Lyceum of the Philippines University– Batangas (LPU-B), Batangas City Philippines. She also published several papers in international journals. She is the Associate Editor of the Asia Pacific Journal of Education, Arts and Sciences (APJEAS) and member of the International Association of Multidisciplinary Research (IAMURE).

Dr. Jake M. Laguador is currently the director, Research and Statistics Center, Lyceum of the Philippines University, Batangas City, Philippines and Research Journal Editor, Lyceum Engineering Research Journal, Lyceum of the Philippines University. He is also the Associate Editor of Asia Pacific Journal of Education, Arts and Science. He has published several papers in reputable international journals.

Dr. Ngozika A. Oleforo iscurrently a Senior Lecturer in the Department of Curriculum Studies, Educational Management and Planning, University of Uyo. An astute scholar who has published several journal articles in referred journals, both in Nigeria and the Overseas. She has receievd several awards due to her contribution in human resources development.

PREFACE

The maiden publication on School E nvironm ent in Nigeria and the Philippines is a welcome development that adds value to a mass and litany of literature which abound in a multidisciplinary field of environmental education in Nigeria and the Philippines. The philosophical conception of the school environment by the World Bank (1974) as a set of complex and totality of physical, geographical, biological, social, cultural and political conjures a generic character of the school environment as a field of study. Appropriately this also fits into M oehlman's (1980) conception of education as "a process which is inherent in all cultures, and expresses itself through material arts, the aesthetic arts, the social arts, cosmology or religion and all forms of communication closely interwoven into every activity." Therefore, environmental education is all pervading.

We are, therefore, not oblivious of the fact that the physical environment of our school buildings and grounds is a key com ponent and fulcrum upon which overall health and safety needs of students, teachers, and visitors to our school environment in both Nigeria and Philippines lie. T he physical environment of our school system should therefore, be jealously guided to free it from the apron string of environmental hazards and challenges so as to enhance healthier learning and research environment

Pertinent policies and protocols should be put in place to ensure that all related pre requisites such as food protection, sanitation, safe w ater supply, healthy and quality good lighting, safe playground, violent prevention and emergency response among other environmental issues, problems and challenges are safeguarded and guaranteed. On the other hand, all levels of government in conjunction with the coalition of agencies and departments of health, hum an resources, and environmental safety etc., should muster resources together and promulgate statutes and rules to regularise and promote good ethics and best practices to engender friendly school environment in both Nigeria and the Philippines.

A study of school environment of two developing countries of Nigeria and the Philippines provides a diagnostic analysis that will enable the reading public ascertain the strengths and weaknesses of education sector in the two countries. It also provides the springboard for cross cutting of ideas by experts and practitioners on wide range of topical issues in environmental education and other related disciplines in both Nigeria and the Philippines. The impact of reform initiative adopted to sharpen the raw edges of the inherent short comings and the quest to seek a panacea to foster functional structure and development of the school environment in the tw o countries is critically examined in this publication.

All the articles thematically assembled to address the ramifications of school environment in Nigeria and the Philippines w ent through insightful scrutiny of international peer reviewers.

Akpanim N. Ekpe Ph.D, FCPA, fnard
Professor of Practice, Public Administration and Local Government
Editor-in-Chief

ACKNOWLEDGMENTS

The onerous challenges in packaging this publication have indebted us to a good number of individuals and institutions. We acknowledge the ingenuity of Dr. Princewill Ikechukwu Egwuasi of the University of Uyo, Nigeria, who first conceived the idea of the book project. It was at his instance that I am conscripted to serve as chief editor of this book project. Being a visioner and protagonist, it is befitting, therefore, to acknowledge him as a coordinator of this book project. I also acknowledge other editors; Dr. Imelda L. An and Dr. Jake M. Laguadr of the Lyceum University of the Philippines, and Dr. Ngozika Oleforo of the University of Uyo, Uyo for all the editorial efforts and scholarly prowess.

The chief editor is grateful to the various tertiary and higher institutions of learning both in Nigeria and the Philippines. They have no doubt provided the needed nitty-gritty in terms of support and encouragement. It is optimistic that this being a maiden one in the series of the envisaged publication, it is hoped that subsequent endeavours in this sphere would equally receive their full and unalloyed support and patronage.

The chief editor has also commended and enjoyed the understanding of the publishing consultant Mr. David Bell and outfit, Author House, Bloomington, IN 47403, USA which has decided to offer the services at commensurate terms and conditions.

Finally, the chief editor is appreciative of the numerous efforts of all the chapter contributors to this publication and wishes to thank them immensely for their courage and commitment in sharing their know-how and expertise on the various themes with the research community. Surely, it is pertinent to state that the views expressed in the chapters are exclusively those of the authors.

Akpanim N. Ekpe PhD, FCPA, fnard
Professor of Practice, Public Adm inistration and Local Go vernm ent
Edito r-in-Ch ief

LIST OF CONTRI BUTORS

Prof. Akpanim N. E kpe, FCP A, fnard
Dean, Faculty of Social and M anagement Sciences
Akw a Ibom State University
Obio Akpa Campus
Akw a Ibom State
Nigeria

Imelda L. An PhD
Dean of the College of E ducation, Arts and Sciences
Lyceum of the Philippines U niversity – Batangas

Jake M. L aguador PhD
Lyceum of the Philippines U niversity,
Batangas City,
Philippines

Ngozika. A. Oleforo, PhD Department
of Curriculum Studies, Educational
Management and Planning University
of Uyo, U yo
Nigeria

Princewill I. Egw uasi, PhD
Information and Public Relations
University of Uyo, U yo
Akw a Ibom State
Nigeria

Chiaka P. Denw igwe, PhD
Psychology Department
FCT College of Education
Zuba Abuja
Nigeria

Flora V. Javier, Ed.D
Lyceum of the Philippines U niversity,
Batangas City,
Philippines

Inua Magaji
Isa Kaita College of Education
Katsina State
Nigeria

Samuel Jeremiah PhD
Department of Curriculum and Instruction
Federal C ollege of Education (Technical)
P.M.B. 11, O moku
Rivers State
Nigeria

Prof. Jane I. Alamina
Department of Science E ducation
Rivers State University of Science and Technology
Nkpolu Port Harcourt
Rivers State
Nigeria

Anthony C. Nwagbara,
Department of Mathematics
School of Sciences
Cross River State College of Education, A kamkpa,
Nigeria.

Mark D. Otarigho
Department of Integrated Science,
College of Education
Warri
Delta State
Nigeria

Edidiong Akpan-Atata, PhD, CLN
Akw a Ibom State University Library
Obio Akpa C ampus,
Akw a Ibom State
Nigeria

Umar A. Abubakar
Department of Science Education,
Faculty of Technology E ducation,
Abubakar Tafaw a Balewa University, Bauchi
Bauchi State
Nigeria

Udua kobong O scar PhD
Univ ersity of Uyo Library
Univ ersity of Uyo, U yo
Akw a Ibo m S tate
Nigeria

Agba je A. Agbaje PhD
Department of Educational Foun dations
Guid ance and Counselling
Univ ersity of Uyo, U yo
Akw a Ibo m S tate
Nigeria

Esmenia R. Javier, MMT, MBA, PhD
Lyceum of the Philippines University- Batangas.
Batan gas City,
Philippines

Patricia N. Eghagha
Department of Integrated Science,
College of Education,
Warri,
Delta State,
Nigeria.

Joy -Telu Hamilton-Ek eke PhD
Department of Teach er Education,
Niger Delta U niversity, Wilb erforce Island,
Bayelsa State,
Nigeria,

Henry D. Katniy on PhD
Integ rated Science Department
Federal C ollege of Education Pankshin
Plateau State
Nigeria

Pew at Z. Duguryil PhD
Chemistry Department
Federal College of Education Pankshin
Plateau State
Nigeria

Martha I. Bulus
Agricultural Science Department
Federal C ollege of Education Pankshin
Plateau State
Nigeria

Helen N. Odiyoma
College of Education
Warri
Delta State
Nigeria

Diep riye Okodoko PhD,
Faculty of Education
Niger Delta University
Wilb erforce Island
Bayelsa S tate
Nigeria

Anderson P. Sele PhD
Faculty of Education
Niger Delta University
Wilberforce Island
Bayelsa State
Nigeria

Ebitimi G. Bekebo
Faculty of Education
Niger Delta University
Wilberforce Island
Bayelsa State
Nigeria

GUIDELINES FOR AUTHORS

The Project Co-ordinator and Board of Editors welcome scholarly articles on Contemporary Issues in School System of Nigeria and the Philippines for publication in its 2nd edition of a book titled, "SCHOOL ENVIRONMENT IN NIGERIA AND THE PHILIPPINES". It is an international book with editors from University of Uyo, Lyceum of the Philippines University-Batangas and Akwa Ibom State University, which aims at showcasing the educational system of the two countries.

Interested contributors are to abide by the following instructions;

- Submit an online copy of manuscript(s), including abstract and references, in MS Word format to prikeg@yahoo.com.
- The title page of the article should carry the authors' names, status/rank and address, place of work and affiliations.
- Abstract of not more than 250 words.
- Manuscripts are received on the understanding that they are original and unpublished works of the author(s) not considered for publication elsewhere.
- Current APA style of referencing should be maintained.
- Author(s) e-mail addresses and phone numbers should accompany the paper.
- Figures, tables, charts and drawings should be clearly drawn and the position marked in the text.
- Pay a publication fee of N30,000 only for Nigerians and $150.00 only for non-Nigerians.
- All manuscripts should reach the Project Co-ordinator on or before 30th June, 2015.

Dr. Princewill I. Egwuasi
Information and Public Relations
University of Uyo, Uyo Akwa Ibom State Nigeria
prikeg@yahoo.com

+2348038955075,
+2348094454419

TABLE OF CONTENTS

THE LEAD CHAPTER

1

MANAGEMENT ISSUES

2

3

4

CURRICULUM ISSUES

5

COUNSELLING ISSUES

12

13

QUALITY ASSURANCE ISSUES

14

15

16

HEALTH AND SAFETY ISSUES

17

ENTREPRENEURSHIP ISSUE

THE LEAD CHAPTER

1

Environmental Problems and Management of Education Systems: An Overview of Nigeria and the Philippines

Prof. Akpanim N. Ekpe *FCPA, fnard*

Introduction

The development process in Nigerian society involves conscious efforts to change present conditions to those which are considered politically, socially and economically desirable. This requires a general transformation of society so that it is able to bring about and to accept change. For this process to take place in earnest, the human resource or work force is a central factor. Therefore, sound and relevant education of the individual is fundamental. It is through educational process that a society tries to inculcate in its on-coming generations skills, desirable values and a world view that are necessary in tackling social and environmental problems facing society and the individual.

A sorry state of Nigeria's public educational system (Nigerian News, October 25th, 2010) can best be described as a "paradox of trial and error, and the blending of tradition with modernity" (Ekpe 2006:53-68). Okebukola (2013:260-296) describes our deplorable educational system as being characterised by high illiteracy rate, low primary education enrolment, decayed infrastructure, restive and frequent striking staff of tertiary institutions and poor quality graduates. Indeed, there has been a problem of a paradigm shift from the inherited colonial system of education which focus departed from the National aspirations and yearnings of the people. The system merely introduced the people to alien culture and tradition. Attempt to reform the old fashion or Westernised system of education is seen in the spates of reforms and reorganizations that Nigeria's educational sector witnessed prior to the attainment of independence in 1960. The reform and reorganization initiative started with Ashby Commission of 1959 which set a platform for the expansion of educational facilities, based on existing financial and manpower constraints of the country. However, the envisaged expansion as postulated by Ashby commission for primary education mainly in the Northern part of Nigeria could not be achieved. The commission's target of 50% enrolment by 1970 could not be made, rather a paltry enrolment of 25% was attained by 1972 (Federal Republic of Nigeria Public Service Main Report 1974).

This chapter examines some environmental problems and management of education system in Nigeria. A brief overview of the Philippines' situation will be attempted.

Study locations
Nigeria

The Federal Republic of Nigeria, is a federal Constitutional Republic comprising 36 states and its Federal Capital Territory, Abuja. Nigeria is located in West Africa and shares land borders with the Republic of Benin in the west, Chad and Cameroon in the east, and Niger in the north. Its coast in the south lies on the Gulf of Guinea in the Atlantic Ocean.

The site of many ancient kingdoms and empires, the modern political state of Nigeria has its origins in the British colonization of the region during the late nineteenth to early twentieth centuries; it emerged from the combination of two neighboring British protectorates: the Southern Nigeria Protectorate and Northern Nigeria Protectorate. During the colonial period, the British set up administrative and legal structures whilst retaining traditional chiefdoms. Nigeria achieved independence in 1960, but plunged into civil war several years later. It has since alternated between democratically elected civilian governments and military dictatorships, with its 2011 presidential elections being viewed as the first to be conducted reasonably freely and fairly.

Nigeria is often referred to as the "Giant of Africa", due to its large population and economy. With approximately 174 million inhabitants, Nigeria is the most populous country in Africa and the seventh most populous country in the world. The country is inhabited by over 500 ethnic groups, of which the three largest are the Hausa, Igbo and Yoruba. Regarding religion, Nigeria is roughly divided in half between Christians, who live mostly in the southern and central parts of the country, and Muslims, concentrated mostly in the northern and southwestern regions. A minority of the population practice religions indigenous to Nigeria, such as those native to Igbo and Yoruba peoples (UNDP, 2014).

Philippines

The Philippines officially known as the Republic of the Philippines is a sovereign island country in Southeast Asia situated in the western Pacific Ocean. It consists of 7,107 Islands that are categorized broadly under three main geographical divisions: Luzon, Visayas, and Mindanao. Its capital city is Manila while its most populous city is Quezon City; both are part of Metro Manila.

To the north of the Philippines across the Luzon Strait lies Taiwan; Vietnam sits west across the South China Sea; southwest is the island of Borneo across the Sulu Sea, and to the south the Celebes Sea separates it from other islands of Indonesia; while to the east it is bounded by the Philippine Sea and the island-nation of Palau. Its location on the Pacific Ring of Fire and close to the equator makes the Philippines prone to earthquakes and typhoons, but also endows it with abundant natural resources and some of the world's greatest biodiversity. At approximately 300,000 square kilometers (115,831 sq mi), the Philippines is the 64th-largest country in the world.

With a population of about 100 million people, the Philippines is the seventh-most populated country in Asia and the 12th most populated country in the world. An additional 12 million Filipinos live overseas, comprising one of the world's largest diasporas. Multiple ethnicities and cultures are found throughout the islands. (Wikipedia, 2014)

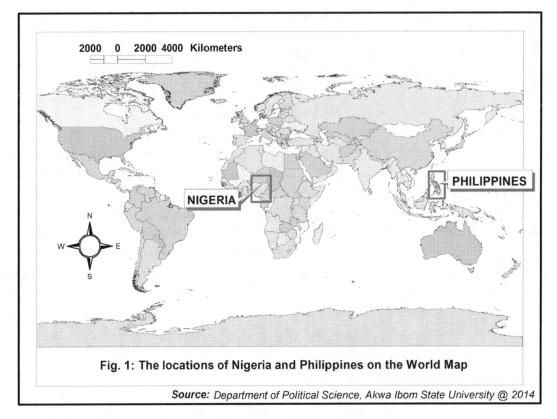

Fig. 1: The locations of Nigeria and Philippines on the World Map

Source: Department of Political Science, Akwa Ibom State University @ 2014

Fig. 1: The locations of Nigeria and Philippines on the world map.

Conceptualization and Theoretical Discourse

Management and education are two interrelated concepts, which are very germane to this discourse. While management and administration can be used interchangeably, management is concerned with the process of planning, organizing, staffing, directing and controlling the operations of various organizations, including education. On the other hand, education according to Iloputaife and Maduewesi (2006) is "a process by which people acquire cultural heritage, knowledge, ideals, and the civilization of the feature". Essentially, therefore, education can be regarded as a means by which the individual is developed so that he will be able to live effectively and efficiently in the present society and make useful contribution to national development. The concept of management of education system therefore, implies the art of educating personnel in the techniques of planning, organizing, staffing, directing and controlling the operations of an organization including education sector. As used in the vernacular or a loosely context, it is an act of training, retraining, and educating personnel in major functional areas of an organization, such as entrepreneurship, personnel and management (Ejiofor 2009:115-116).

The theoretical orientation upon which this chapter relies is based on Munro's (1966) conception of education in which he relates education to a process of social organization. To him, education has three purposes. First, to give young men and women the sort of training which will enable them better to earn their own living. Second, to develop the personality of the individual. It is the function of the school to search out the native abilities and inclinations of each pupil so that these qualities may be trained and developed. The third purpose which is regarded as topmost, is the realisation of public education as having the potentialities of impacting training in good citizenship. This is compelling and needed in democratic settings and rests upon the good sense and tolerance of other people. It is the social purpose of education to train men and women to think before they speak or act, to remember that there are two sides to every situation and hence to approach public issues without discrimination (Munro 1966).

Environmental Issues and Problems in Nigeria's Education System

Nigerian environmental issues in Education are indeed multifarious and contentious, which directly or indirectly impinge on education in the country. Such issues cut across diverse spectrum of endeavours of our society and are therefore, contemporary subject matters which engage the attention and minds of the generality of the people and government. Therefore, Nigerian environmental issues are the most important aspect of situational discourse of this chapter.

President Olusegun Aremu Obasanjo led administration has made system wide reforms in educational sector, including strategic intervention which led to apparent increase in literacy rate from 48.9% to 63.2% in 2006. The Table 1 herein shown clearly depicts the situation between1990-2006.

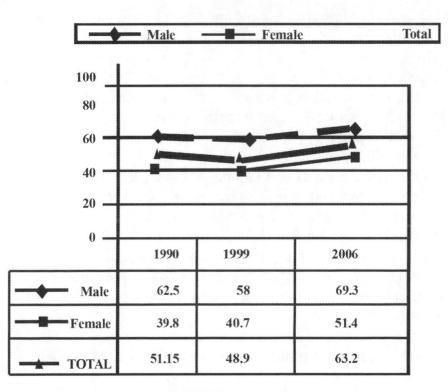

	1990	1999	2006
Male	62.5	58	69.3
Female	39.8	40.7	51.4
TOTAL	51.15	48.9	63.2

Fig. 2: Trends in Adult Literacy Ratio (1990-2006)

Data Source Federal Ministry of Education (FME) and Federal Office of Statistics (FOS) Digests of Statistics.
UNESCO World Education Report, 1990, 1997, 2006
Multiple Indicator Cluster Survey

Structural Overview of Nigeria's and the Philippines' Education Systems

The introduction of 6-3-3-4 Education Reform in Nigeria though alien to the country and a brain child of Late Babs Fafunwa was supposed to be a comprehensive masterpiece that was intended to give free educational access to people of school age and to emphasize their trainability. The three years allocated for JSS 1-3 now called Basic Education is grossly inadequate to provide the pupils with the basic requirements needed to make them trainable and self-reliant in the labour market. Besides, the implementation of the system has not remedied the fallen standard of education in the country. The system is criticised for being a by-product or responsible for the weak primary education system as it produces weak and poor students for the secondary schools, which are no better either, and so the chain of mediocrity continues up to the higher education level and the circle completes itself with the garbage led back into the society with serious implication for national competitiveness (Nigerian News 2010).

A sister country of Sierra Leone which adopted the same 6-3-3-4 system had long abandoned it and replaced it with 6-3-4-4 system which translates into additional years of Secondary School education. A country such as Philippines also allocates six years for Nigeria's Jss1-3 basic equivalent. Thus, both Sierra Leone and Philippines Education systems offer accommodative opportunities for both the bright and the average pupils and give every child an opportunity to be useful to the society through offer of a more conducive environment. There is an inbuilt assumption that every child will compulsorily go to school up to the Junior Secondary School level. Again, while the Philippines educational system is decentralised, managed and regulated by the Department of Education, that of Nigeria is a shared responsibility among the three tiers of government, namely Federal, State, and Local. On September 24, 1972, through the Presidential Decree No. 1, the Department of Education, Culture and Sports Council was decentralised with decision-making shared among thirteen regional offices. In terms of structure, the Education Act of 1982 provided for an integrated system of education covering both formal and non-formal education at all levels. Section 29 of the Act sought to upgrade education institution's standards to achieve "quality education" through voluntary accreditation for schools, colleges, and Universities. It is the Department of Education in Philippines that exercises sole superintendence over the educational system (Both public and private) including the preparation of the curriculum used in schools, and allocation of funds. It also regulates the construction of schools and other educational facilities and the recruitment of teachers and staff. For sure, in 2011, Philippines started transition from its old 10years basic educational system to 12 years educational system as mandated by the Department of education. The new 12 years system is now compulsory along with the adoption of a new curriculum for all schools. The transition period is targeted to end with 2017-2018 school year which is the graduation date designed for the first corps of graduates who entered the new educational system in the country.

The Environmental Issues

- **School Management**

The Headmasters and Principals of the Primary and Secondary schools as managers represent the first tier in the school management system. They perform such routine tasks as organization of duty schedules and tasks, supervision of staff and ensure their regular payment of salaries, etc. Notwithstanding their enormous responsibilities, most of them are not given proper care and attention in terms of training and retraining on the job. We, therefore, advocate that management roles and tasks of heads of schools be recognised and they should be given relevant training to enable them cope systematically with their managerial and leadership responsibilities.

- **The Mismatch between Quality and Quantity of Primary School Enrolment Disposition**

The quality and quantity in primary education disposition in Nigeria shows that the level of numeracy competence and result of literacy test is unimpressive and significant inequality exists between urban and rural areas, as well as between private and public institutions. This scenario is attributable to Government's inability to tackle the problem of quality in the school system through reforms and changes in curriculum, increase in teacher-pupil-ratio, and the use of continuous assessment scores or promotion from one class level to another. This is contrary to what obtains in Philippines, where the Department of Education controls and moderates activities, including curriculum standardization.

- **Infrastructure**

Acute dearth of infrastructure in our school system generally has destabilizing effects both on physical and academic effectiveness of our school system. The existing handicaps and constraints which are most worrisome require prompt attention by all stake holders in our educational system, including governments at all levels which should play catalyst roles. The infrastructural deficiencies are:

(a) Shortage of staff (both teaching and non-teaching)
(b) Shortage of Materials to include books and journals, teaching resources and aids and computers.
(c) Absence of industrial exposure: The existing arrangement for giving students industrial work experience has many defects. Three of these are:
    i.   Insufficient positions or openings for placement
    ii.   Short work period
    iii. Inadequate supervision.

- **Inconsistency in Education Policy**

One of the crucial issues facing Nigeria's educational system in the 21st Century is apparent inconsistency and incoherency in educational policy. The policy inconsistency etc. has indeed thwarted the structure and effectiveness in service delivery of both Primary and Secondary layers of our entire educational system. It is therefore advocated that in order to catch up with the expectation of the demands of globalization and the year 2020, Nigeria needs to strengthen or reinvigorate her educational policy to enable her join the league of other developed countries of the world in 2020 and beyond.

- **Acknowledgement of NUC/TETFUND's Infrastructural Intervention Strategies**

It is pertinent to commend the critical intervention of the National University Commission and Education Trust Fund (NUC / ETF) for rescuing our University system from many years of infrastructural decay. Since 2001, there has been tremendous financial improvement in the funding of tertiary institutions in the country. Through NUC / Education Trust Fund, many Nigerian Universities, Polytechnics, colleges of education, etc. have benefitted from direct interventions in the areas of infrastructural development of these institutions. For instance, during President Obasanjo's led administration, the level of funding both for recurrent and capital expenditure in these institutions has increased with the provision of National digital library facilities to guarantee availability of current books and Journals for University students and staff (Okebukola, 2013). By 2007, there has also been significant improvement in both primary school enrolment and physical facilities across the length and breadth of the country. Twenty five million pupils was recorded in 2007 and twenty nine thousand classroom blocks were constructed. Thus, by May 2007, a total of forty eight thousand classroom blocks were constructed. It is optimistic that this momentum will persist in future. At the higher education level, a success story is equally resounding. The number of Colleges of Education, Polytechnics, and Universities has increased from 204 in 1999 to 310. (**Data source:** Federal Ministry of Education and Federal Office of Statistics 1990-2006)

Conclusion

Even though environmental problems which plague our educational system are multifarious, they are in no way insurmountable. Education is a capital intensive enterprise which should not be left alone for government. It is the responsibility of all. Therefore, the expected gains or returns of education may remain elusive if the ever teeming expectations of citizens are not matched with appropriate resources, infrastructure and environment.

Therefore, the sustainability of our educational system will depend greatly on the coalition and network of all stakeholders, lessons to be learned from other sister countries and donor partners that Nigeria can muster and mobilize.

References

Ejiofor, P. (2009). *Management in Nigeria: Theories and Issues. Enugu:* Africana FEP Publishers Plc, pp 131-135

Ekpe, A. (2006). *Parliamentarianism in Nigeria: An Odyssey in the Niger Delta.* A Publication of Local Government in Nigeria. (ALGON) – Uyo pp 52 – 58

Iloputaife, C. and Maduewesi, B. (2006). *Issues and Challenges in Nigeria Education in the 21ˢᵗ Century (Eds).* Onitsha: West & Solomon Publishing Ltd, pp 1-15.

Okebuloka, P. (2013). *Olusegun Obasanjo: The Presidential Legacy (1999-2007) Vol. 1.* Ibadan: Book Craft, pp 260-296.

Federal Republic of Nigeria (1974). *Public Service Commission Main Report: Federal Ministry of Information.* Lagos: Printing Division, pp. 135-146.

Dr. Princewill Egwuasi

http://www.assemblyonline.info. *Nigerian News, (2010) - Reforming Nigeria's educational System.* Retrieved 20th November, 2014.

http://www.wikipedia (2014). Retrieved; 20th November, 2014.

Human Development Report Summary (2014). *United Nations Development Programme,* pp. 21–25. Retrieved; 20th November, 2014.

MANAGEMENT ISSUES

2

Philippine Education System with K to 12 Implementation

Imelda L. An *PhD* & Jake M. Laguador *PhD*

Introduction
Education System in the Philippines

Moving ahead with other countries in South East Asia or even with the first world countries around the globe would not be possible without taking into consideration the quality of education and how the government supports the education system towards the attainment of building a progressive nation.

The education reform that resulted in the K-12 basic education curriculum stems from the need to address the onslaught of globalization and regional cooperation for the graduates of HEIs to be globally competitive. This requires internal changes to include a shift from 10 to 12 years of basic education. The reform is stirred by the sore state of high school education in the country, which has deteriorated in the quality and competencies of its graduates and has poorly prepared High School graduates for college and for the labor market (Quilinguing, 2013).

In the Philippines, the children started in attending school through Kindergarten to prepare the pupils gradually in formal education before entering in Elementary School which is composed of 6 years of compulsory education divided into three (3) years of primary level and another three (3) intermediate level. Secondary education consists of four years in the old system but now in the new curriculum, High School is now composed of six (6) years, where the students should spend four (4) years of Junior High School and two (2) years for Senior High School.

K to 12 is the new curriculum of basic education which means from Kindergarten to Grade 1 to 12. One of the main objectives of this development is to meet the standards of other countries which are implementing 12 years or more of basic education compared to the Philippines with 10 years. Its focus is learner-centered approach where pupils shall be given enough emphasis during the teaching and learning process. The DepEd claimed that with K to 12, students will not have to rush through the lessons anymore. It will also do away with unnecessary topics in the curriculum so that students will develop competencies and acquire life skills that will make them productive members of the society ("K to 12: The Key to Quality Education?" 2011).

K to 12 also aims to provide adequate time for the students to develop their knowledge, skills and attitude towards future employment after graduating from high school where they are more confident to face challenges of the world.

Some of the salient features of this new system are to strengthen the early childhood education of the pupils from universal kindergarten; to make the curriculum relevant to the learners through contextualization and enhancement of curriculum; to ensure integrated and seamless learning through spiral progression; to build proficiency through mother tongue-based multilingual education; and to nurture the holistically developed Filipino ("The K to 12 Basic Education Program").

Students may choose a specialization based on their interest, aptitude and capacity when they reach Senior High School which falls under either the Core Curriculum or Specific tracks. The core curriculum is composed of seven (7) learning areas: Languages, Literature, Communication, Mathematics, Philosophy, Natural Sciences, and Social Sciences while career track is composed of the following: Academic; Technical-Vocational-Livelihood; and Sports and Arts. The academic track includes three strands: Business, Accountancy, Management (BAM); Humanities, Education, Social Sciences (HESS); and Science, Technology, Engineering, Mathematics (STEM). Students undergo immersion, which may include earn-while-you-learn opportunities, to provide them relevant exposure and actual experience in their chosen track ("The K to 12 Basic Education Program").

There will be 31 total subjects required for Senior High School, 15 from the Core Subjects and 16 from track Subjects where this track was broken down into 7 Contextualized subjects and 9 Specialization subjects.

After finishing Grade 10, a student can obtain Certificates of Competency (COC) or a National Certificate Level I (NC I). After finishing a Technical-Vocational-Livelihood track in Grade 12, a student may obtain a National Certificate Level II (NC II), provided he/she passes the competency-based assessment of the Technical Education and Skills Development Authority (TESDA). NC I and NC II improves employability of graduates in fields like Agriculture, Electronics, and Trade ("The K to 12 Basic Education Program").

Technical and vocational education is offered by government operated or private institutions often called colleges. Programs duration varies from a few weeks to 3 years. Upon the graduation from most of the programs, students may take TESDA (Technical Education and Skills Authority) examination to receive an appropriate certificate or diploma ("Education System in the Philippines").

The K-12 program was precisely supposed to either prepare students for gainful work after basic education or prepare students for college. The either/or has become a both/and. It intends both to equip the students with the skills necessary for gainful employment and to prepare them for college within the same time constraint. And because the designers are all college graduates with PhD's from the best of higher educational intentions, but without the experience of training students in handling a lathe or a welding machine, we now have a policy which has effectively shut out meaningful skills development in favor of pre-college preparation. The K-12 program has thereby been reduced to pre-college preparation whose "core curriculum," according to Mr. Elvin Uy, will prepare the student for college according to the College Readiness Standards of the CHED ("Serious Problems with the K-12", 2014).

Effects and Challenges of K to 12 Implementation

The two additional years in High School needs preparation and major adjustment for Department of Education (DepEd) and Commission and Higher Education (CHED) as well as in the administration of Secondary and Tertiary Schools in the country. College Teachers, especially those who are teaching General Education courses, would be affected due to no enrollees for First and Second year college students from School Year (SY) 2016 – 2017 and SY 2017-2018 because these students will be enrolled in Senior High School.

The possible displacement of higher education faculty as a result of the new GE curriculum as well as during the period when students are in Grades 11 and 12 instead of in College is indeed a serious concern. There are remedies being discussed such as the assignment of disciplinal courses to former GE faculty, the deployment of some higher education faculty to senior high school, the grant of research load to deserving faculty, and others. The CHED, in fact, has a technical working group studying the challenges posed by the transition to K12 and is working out alternative solutions with the help of DepEd, Department of Labor and Employment (DOLE) and other concerned agencies ("On the Removal of Filipino", 2014).

Private higher education institutions without secondary school are now establishing high school department to compensate the losses in college enrolees that would occur in 2016. But K to 12 will also provide enrolees to Tertiary education institutions who will serve as partners of Secondary Schools on its implementation due to lack of infrastructure like instructional facilities and laboratories as well as the man power to operate the Grades 11 and 12 on their present state. Instead of building new facilities for this purpose, establishing linkages and tie-ups with HEIs would be more practical to support the implementation of K to 12. HEIs are ready to offer their services and accommodate the concern of basic education since there would be no freshmen enrolees by 2016.

There would be changes in the way higher education institutions offer their curricular programs in terms of its structure especially in general education and years to finish a certain degree in college. The new General Education Curriculum (GEC) has been reduced from 63 units (for humanities and social science majors) or 51 units (for science, engineering and math majors) to 36 units for all students. The 27/15 units removed was not all in Filipino. They also include courses in English, Literature, Math, Natural Sciences, Humanities and Social Sciences. The new GEC, moreover, offers entirely different courses from the old one ("On the Removal of Filipino", 2014). The greatest fear of the General Education faculty members especially those contractual in HEIs is to lose their jobs in 2016 which prompted for some of them to find their way out of the country as initial preparation due to absence of clear plans of the School Administration for them. The same apprehension is being felt by the teachers handling professional courses where they see themselves handling lesser workloads which led for some of them to take Licensure Examination for Teachers to qualify their requirement for high school teaching.

Conclusion

The K-12 Program hopes to decongest the basic education curricula; prepare the students for higher education and for the labor market, and be globally competitive/benchmark with global standards (Quilinguing, 2013). The Philippine Government through DepEd and CHED is very active in disseminating the information regarding the K to 12 implementation. Regional and National conferences and seminars are being held to update the school administrators of Basic Education and Higher Education Institutions on the preparation of new curriculum.

Private and Public HEIs are now starting to review and revise their curricula based on the requirements of K to 12. Instructional materials are also being reviewed to meet the necessary outcomes needed by the new curriculum.

The K to 12 roadmap is still on progress where everyone is working so hard to address the issue of transformation in the Philippine education system which answers to the demand of ASEAN integration. There are critical issues and challenges that need to be addressed immediately by the Philippine Government but it is the role of everyone to take part in providing solutions and be proactive in answering the questions that may arise during the process of implementation rather than making the concerns more problematic.

References

Education System in the Philippines, *http://www.classbase.com/Countries/philippines/Education-System*, date retrieved: November 25, 2014

K to 12: The Key to Quality Education?, (2011), Policy Brief: Senate Economic Planning Office, url; *https://www.senate.gov.ph/publications/PB%202011-02%20-%20K%20to%2012%20The%20Key%20to%20Quality.pdf,* date retrieved: November 26, 2014.

On the Removal of Filipino and Filipino Teachers from the New General Education Curriculum (2014), Press Statement, Commission On Higher Education, url: *http://www.ched.gov.ph/wp-content/uploads/2014/temp/CHED-Statement-on-Filipino.pdf,* date retrieved: November 26, 2014.

Quilinguing, K. (2013). UP Gears up for the Impact of the K-12 Curriculum and ASEAN Economic Cooperation 2015, url: *http://www1.up.edu.ph/index.php/up-gears-up-for-the-impact-of-the-k-12-curriculum-and-asean-economic-cooperation-2015/,* date retrieved: November 26, 2014

Serious Problems with the K-12 Senior High School Curriculum (2014), https://taborasj.wordpress.com/2014/02/18/serious-problems-with-the-k-12-senior-high-school-curriculum/, date retrieved: November 26, 2014.

The K to 12 Basic Education Program, Official Gazette, url: http://www.gov.ph/k-12/, date retrieved: November 26, 2014.

3

Teacher, Classroom Management and Climate Change in Nigeria

Ngozika. A. Oleforo, *PhD*

Abstract

O ne of the major functions of the teacher is effective classroom management as this enhances teaching and learning processes. It eases the stress in attaining educational objectives, especially in this era of varying climatic conditions. Climate change manifests in either increased or decreased temperature, leading to excessive heat or cold which are all capable of causing distraction and disrupting effective teaching and learning. This paper therefore discussed the teacher, classroom management and climate change, causes of climate change, various effects of climate change and their impediments to effective classroom management. It was recommended that teachers should use strategies such as checking weather forecasts for each day, preparing lessons to meet challenges, keeping students actively engaged and actively supervising the classroom.

Introduction

One of the fundamental objectives of the school system is to ensure effective teaching-learning process. As part of measures to achieve this objective, the teacher must be able to manage the classroom effectively. According to Eggen and Kauchak (2007), classroom management is defined as teachers' strategies that create and maintain an orderly learning environment. Classroom management is also defined as the methods and strategies an educator uses to maintain a classroom environment that is conducive to student success and learning (McCreary, 2009). These definitions show that classroom management is all about the strategies or methods used by the teacher to ensure the classroom setting is conducive for learning, and has teachers who are effective, manage their classrooms with procedures and routines. This requires diligence and careful planning. Once the classroom is running smoothly, the teachers will spend less time in attending to disciplinary matters, have more time to teach and positively interact with the students.

The main goal of classroom management is to bring effective teaching and learning. Eggen and Kauchak (2007) identify three major goals of classroom management, these include creating a good classroom climate, maximizing opportunities for learning and developing learner responsibility. Effective classroom management will enhance teaching-learning process. According to Currington (2009), it will bring about consistent routines, effective time management, positive atmosphere, high test scores and students' growth. Young (2010) also maintains that effective classroom management will eliminate disruptive behaviour of students that could impede effective teaching and learning.

There are various factors that militate against effective classroom management. Ajayi (2004) classifies the problems of classroom management into three namely; student, teacher and school factors. According to him, the student factor includes absenteeism, disobedience, fighting, noise, sleeping, and inattentiveness among others. The teacher factor includes poor mastery of the subject matter, laziness, and use of inappropriate methods of instruction, lack of authority in the classroom and inadequate planning and preparation of lessons. The school factor includes large class size, lack of instructional materials, poor school administration and harsh school environment among others. Oghuvbu and Atakpo (2008) also identify students shouting, calling names, sleeping, talking or discussing during lessons as common classroom management problem.

It must be emphasized that the various problems of classroom management could also be induced by climate change. According to Omotayo (2010), climate change is alteration in existing weather condition over a period of time attributed mainly to greenhouse gas emissions and other causes. The manifestation of this change can be seen in the ecology, rainfall pattern, temperature, humidity, human and livestock adaptation (Adedoyin, 2010). Climate change impacts negatively on human beings and their environment. The negative effects of climate change include environmental degradation, poor health, food insecurity, social tension, disruption of social and economic activities, air pollution, and heat waves among others. These problems are inimical to the effective functioning of the school system. They are potential impediments to the teaching-learning process. It therefore becomes imperative for the teacher to use some strategies or techniques in managing the classroom in order to mitigate the negative effects of climate change on classroom setting.

Studies by Ajayi (2013), McCreary (2009), Smith (2009) and Bora (2010) have shown that there are various techniques which the teacher could use to manage the classroom. These techniques include good knowledge of the learners; good mastery of the subject matter; use of appropriate methods of instruction; motivation; discipline; provision of instructional materials and manageable class size. Others include respect, consistency, proximity, seating arrangement, student participation in lessons and making concrete rules. The teacher must understand the peculiarities of his or her classroom setting and the school environment and must be professionally competent in using the various techniques to manage the classroom in order to ensure effective teaching and learning. The importance of classroom and its management necessitated the writing of this paper especially in this era of climate change in Nigeria and the world over.

The Concept of Classroom Management

Classroom management as a concept has been defined in various ways. The classroom, according to Atanda (2008) is a room where a class of pupils/students having similar characteristics is taught. It is a geographical space occupied by a group of students. It can be defined as a room set aside and specifically designed and furnished for the purpose of teaching and learning. Classroom management on the other hand involves the organization, maintenance and utilization of the various components of the classroom to enhance teaching and learning. Arogundele (2008) refers to classroom management as some forms of arrangement and coordination that go on in the classroom. Adewale and Yoloye (1994) defined classroom management as the process whereby human and material resources are organized, students motivated and inspired and a cooperative working environment created to accomplish educational goals. Classroom management can be said to be a bringing together in a careful manner those element which help create good teaching and learning environment in a class.

From the foregoing, it is established that the creator and motivator of classroom management is the teacher. Classroom management in climate change therefore refers to the process of getting teaching-learning activities accomplished while facing climatic change problems. Classroom management refers to method or techniques which a teacher adopts to ensure every learner utilizes available resources with the sole aim of achieving the goals of the school system towards learning. Orukokan and Oladipo (1994) also defined classroom management as bringing together in a careful manner those elements that help create good teaching-learning conditions in class. According to Oleforo (2014), classroom management refers to all activities put in place by the teacher and the school heads to ensure effective teaching-learning process in the classroom. Such activities include mastery of the subject matter, making the classroom environment conducive for learning, using appropriate methods, knowing the students with regards to their ability, interest and deficiencies, among others.

Classroom management refers to everything a teacher does to organize students, space, time and materials so that instructions and students' learning can take place. The essence of classroom management is to ensure effective teaching-learning process. A meta-analysis of the past 50 years of classroom research identifies classroom management as the most important factor, even above student aptitude, affecting student learning.

What is Climate Change?

The term climate refers to the average weather condition at a particular place over a long period of time. Therefore any change that occurs in the weather condition is referred to as climatic change. Climatic change has been defined in various ways. Ayoade (2003), Tamuno (2004) and Tamuno (2007) defined climate change as variations in climate over a long period that helps to discern a shift in the climatic characteristics of a place for about 100 years without reversing to former characteristics. Climate change is also defined as a change in the average weather that a given region experiences. Average weather includes all the features we associate with the weather such as temperature, wind patterns and precipitation (Natural Resources Canada, 2007). IPCC (2007) defines climate change as a change in the state of the climate that can be identified (e.g

19

by using statistical tests) by changes in the main and/or the variability of its properties which persists for an extended period typically decades or longer.

Climate change is different from global warming but they are closely related. Global warming refers to rising global temperature which causes climate to change. Warmer global temperatures in the atmosphere and oceans lead to climate change affecting rainfall patterns, storms and droughts, growing seasons, humidity, sea level. Global warming is worldwide, climate change can occur at the global, continental, regional and local levels. Moreover, while a warming trend is global, different areas around the world experience different specific changes in their climates.

Causes of Climate Change

Studies by Ojo, Ojo and Oni (2001), and Tamuno (2009) have shown that there are two major causes of climate change namely anthropogenic and natural causes which actually bring about climate in the ratio of about 60:40.

Anthropogenic causes refer to activities that either emit large amount of greenhouse gases such as carbondioxide (CO_2), methane (CH_4), sulphur dioxide (SO_2), etc into the atmosphere that depletes the ozone layer or activities that reduce the atmosphere. Activities of man that emit large amounts of greenhouse gases (GHGS) include industrialization, burning of fossil fuel, gas flaring, urbanization and agriculture. On the other hand, activities such as deforestation, alterations in land use, water pollution and agricultural practices reduce the amount of carbon absorbed from the atmosphere. Since the advent of industrial revolution, man-made activities have added significant quantities of GHGS to the atmosphere. The atmospheric concentrations of carbon dioxide, methane and nitrous oxide have grown by about 31%, 151% and 17% respectively between 1750 and 2000 (IPCC, 2001).

Climate changes that are attributed to nature are referred to as a natural cause. According to Oleforo, Amaechi, and Nwachukwu (2013), the natural causes of climate changes are classified into three namely:

a. Terrestrial (Earth) causes induced through changes in:
   - The earths topography
   - The atmospheric chemistry and
   - Ecosphere
b. Astronomical causes induced through changes in:
   - The eccentricity of the earth's orbit
   - The procession of the equinoxes
   - The obliquity of the plane of ecliptic
c. Extraterrestrial causes affected through change in:
   - Variations in solar radiation amount
   - Variations in the absorption of solar radiation outside the earth's atmosphere.

Effects of Climate Change

Adelekan (2009) identifies the major level of impacts to include damage to roads, disruptions of movement, dirty environment, flooding of community and school children being prevented going to school. The household level impacts include damage to deterioration of building infrastructures, flooded houses and rooms, prevalence of malaria, lack of potable water, homelessness,, destruction of household properties and diseases. The individual level impacts include poor health status, disruption of economic and livelihood activities and scarcity of food.

In another development, DFLD (2009) reveals that climate change will impact negatively on Nigeria's economy particularly in the areas of agriculture, water and power while the Millennium Development Goals to reduce hunger and poverty and to establish environmental sustainability will be much more difficult to achieve. It further identified the poor, the old, women, children and those in agriculture as the most vulnerable with relatively severe outcomes.

Similarly, Ikpi (2010) identifies the impact of climate change on Nigeria to include loss in GDP, inability to attain the MDGs particularly on hunger and poverty and environmental sustainability, land loss, food insecurity, social tensions, energy crisis, diseases damaged transport routes, among others. Fasona and Omojola (2005) also report that majority of the communal clashes in Nigeria were caused by environmental degradation arising from climate change.

The effects of climate change on Niger Delta include soil fertility loss, decreased agricultural yield, deforestation, fishery resource decline, flooding and coastal/marine erosion and health decline (Chinweze and Abiola-Oloke, (2009). Etuonovbe (2007) also identifies natural disasters, reduction in the water available for drinking and washing, food insecurity, heat waves, air pollution; social dislocation, infectious diseases and erosion as effects of climate change. Some health problems have also been attributed to climate change. According to Omigbodun (2010), such health problems include but not limited to diarrhea, malaria, cholera, typhoid, hypertension, hepatitis A virus and low sperm counts.

Effects of Climate Change on Classroom Management

The various effects of climate change such as flooding, drought, food insecurity, diseases, environmental degradation, fall in GDP, social tension etc. have implications on classroom management. Climate change could affect classroom management in the following ways:
- Students indiscipline in the classroom
- Absenteeism of students in the school
- Lack of motivation of students in the school
- Inadequate participation of pupils during lesson
- Short of infrastructural materials and other facilities in the school
- Rowdy classroom

- Disruption of teaching activities
- Poor instructional delivery
- Inability of students to cope with learning activities as a result of illness
- Laziness

It therefore becomes necessary for teachers to mitigate the effects of climate change on classroom management.

Strategies for Classroom Management in Climate Change

In order to mitigate the negative effect of climate change on teaching-learning process, teachers must use some strategies in managing the classroom to ensure effective instructional delivery. The strategies are examined as follows:

- Checking weather forecast for each day. Weather forecast is a prediction about the specific atmospheric condition, expected of a location in the short-term which is usually hours to days. Teachers have to check the weather forecasts for each day, through radio, television or reading newspapers. Teachers' knowledge of the weather forecast for each day will make them pro-active in planning the classroom activities for each day. For instance, if the weather for the day is going to be hot, lessons scheduled for the afternoon period must be such that should not focus on difficult or complex topics. If there is going to be heavy rains during the lesson periods, the pupils could be engaged in classroom assignments to keep them busy and make them behave well during the periods.
- Well-prepared lessons to meet challenges; it is necessary for the teacher to prepare his/her lesson plan well in order to meet the challenges of climate change. A lesson plan is a resume of what is going to be done in a lesson. It indicates clearly what is going to happen during the course of a lesson. It should not be too sketchy such as to gloss over important details and contents and it should not run into several pages that look unwieldy to handle. The lesson plan should contain vital information that can enhance effective instructional delivery. Such information includes preliminary information, previous knowledge, objectives, introduction and presentation of the lesson, evaluation, summary and assignment. For the purpose of meeting the challenges of climate change, lesson plan should be student-centered such that they are actively involved in the lesson. In order to ensure adequate participation of pupils in the lesson, their expected activities must be able to enhance the attainment of the objectives of the lesson.
- Keeping students actively engaged; harsh effects of climate change could make students restless, passive and uncoordinated during the teaching-learning process. It is the responsibility of the teacher to engage the students actively in the lessons. This can be done in various ways. The teacher must ensure the students are attentive and the step-by-step presentation of the lesson must be

closely related to the experience of the students as much as possible. Moreover, they must participate in the lesson through questioning, demonstration, clarification of issues or ideas, contribution to discussion, experimentation and practice exercises among others. Moreover, the presentation of the lesson must be sequential and pleasant. The teacher should also make adequate provision for the individual differences during the lesson and must readily be at alert to students problems.

• Reinforcing appropriate behaviour; there are some inappropriate behaviour which impede effective teaching process. Such behaviour include murmuring, disturbing others and teachers, loneliness, withdrawal, depression, aggression, opposition, severe bullying, violence, truancy. These behaviours could be precipitated by climate change. It therefore becomes necessary for the teacher to reinforce appropriate behaviour of the students by maintaining discipline in the classroom and actively engage the students in the lesson. The teacher must also be friendly but firm to the students. He or she finds desirable and wants more of it. Appropriate behaviour of the students includes attentiveness, participation in the lesson, obedience to classroom rules and regulations, tolerance, love and cooperation.

• Actively supervising the classroom; as a result of the various negative effects of climate change, students may be noisy, aggressive, bored, hyperactive, passive, and disenchanted. To this end, their activities in the classroom may not be supportive of effective teaching and learning. Hence, the teacher must actively supervise students' activities in the classroom in order to ensure unity of purpose and sense of direction among them during the teaching-learning process. For teachers to actively supervise classroom activities of students, he or she should set and implement classroom rules and regulations to maintain discipline, he or she should move round the classroom using the regulations to maintain discipline, he or she should move round the classroom using the 'roving patrol' technique. Moreover, he or she should adopt the 'roving eye' approach to the surveillance of all members of the class and ensure a continual overview of the activities of all individual students or groups of students. The teacher should also be sensitive to students' problems in the classroom and address them appropriately.

• Motivating the students for learning; motivation is a force, drive or urge that makes one do what one is aroused to do. It is an energizer or driving force of man's action. Motivation helps to describe the needs, drive, wishes, desires and other associate forces which propels the individual towards set goals. The various effects of climate change on teaching-learning process make it mandatory for the teacher to motivate students to learn. Where students are not motivated, teaching may occur without learning. It therefore becomes imperative for the teacher to adopt various methods of motivating the students towards learning. Some of the methods that can be used by the teachers include maintaining cordial relationship with the students; ensuring the classroom environment is safe and suitable for effective teaching-learning process and using various methods of instruction to stimulate and induce students to learn better. Others include making every student feel important and encouraging him or her to participate in the lesson; rewarding good work or performance through open commendation, presentation of gifts and prizes; making the students know the level of their performance as and when due and encourage learners to direct their learning feeling of success.

Conclusion

The major objective of classroom management is to ensure effective teaching-learning process. However, this cannot be easily accomplished in an environment that is not conducive for learning as a result of negative effects of climate change, health-related challenges like illness, aggression, depression, loneliness, truancy, restlessness and insubordination. It therefore becomes expedient for teachers to evolve some strategies for managing the classroom in order to mitigate the negative effects of climate change. Such strategies include checking weather forecasts for each day, well-prepared lessons to meet challenges, keeping students actively engaged, reinforcing appropriate students' behaviour, actively supervising the classroom, and motivating students for learning.

References

Adedoyin, S. F. (2010). *Good governance: Implication for climate change, food security and rural development in Nigeria.* Maiden edition of the faculty of Agricultural Sciences. Public lecture series. University of Ado-Ekiti, Nigeria.

Adelekan (2009).Vulnerability of poor urban coastal communities to climate change in Lagos, Nigeria. Fifth Urban Symposuim. *http//www.silereresources.worldbank. org/INTURBANDEVELOPMENT/.../Adelakan.pdf.* Retrieved 10th October, 2014.

Adewale, E. E. & Yoloye, M. U. (1994). Classroom management. In W. Osisiawo (Ed.), *Education for the Nigerian Certificate in Education (Vol. 1).* Ibadan: Alalas Nigeria Company.

Ajayi, I. A. (2004). *Social Science Methods.* Ado-Ekiti: Greenline Publishers.

Arogundele, B. B. (2008). Classroom management in education in J. C. Babalola & A. O. Ayeni (Eds)., *Educational management: Theories and tasks.* Lagos: Macmillan Nigeria Publishers Limited.

Atanda, A. I. (2008). Classroom Management in Education. In J. C. Babalola & A. O. Ayeni (Eds). *Educational Management: Theories and tasks.* Lagos Macmillan Nigeria Publishers Limited.

Ayoade, J. O. (2003). *Climate Change.* Ibadan: Vantage Publishers.

Chinweze, C. & Abiola, O. (2009). Women issues, poverty and social challenge in the Nigerian Niger Delta context. *A paper presented at IHDP open meeting, the 7th international conference on Human Dimension of Global Environment change. 26th – 30th April, UN Campus, Bonn Germany.*

Currington, L. (2009). Importance of classroom management. *http://www.whaw.com/about542/809 important classroom management.html.* Retrieved 11th September, 2014.

DFID (2009). Impact of climate change on Nigeria's economy. Final report *http://www/pak Nigeria.org/.../27 impact of climate_change_on_Nigeria's economy.* Retrieved 15th September, 2010.

Eggen, P. & Kauchak, D. (2007). *Educational psychology.* Columbus: Pearson Prentice Hall.

Etuonovbe, A. K. (2007). Coastal settlement and climate changes. The effects of climate changes sea level rise on the people of Awoye in Ondo State, Nigeria. Strategic integration of surveying services.FIGR working week. Hong Kong SAR, China, 13-17 May. *http//www.fig.net/pub/fig2007/papers/ts_8/fts_03_ettunovbe.* Retrieved 15th October, 2014.

Fasona, M. J. & Omojola, A. S. (2005).Climate change, human security and communal clashes in Nigeria. *Paper presented at International Workshop on Human Security and Climate Change; Holmen Fjord Hotel near Osolo 21-23 June.*

Ikpi, A. (2010). The Nigeria economy and climate change. A paper presented at NASS capacity building workshop on climate change. Jan. 4. *http//www.naspanigeria.org/.../27. Impact of climate on Nigeria's economy.* Retrieved on 18th August, 2014.

IPCC (2007). Climate changes. The fourth assessment report (AR4). Synthesis report of policy makers. *http://www.IPCC.ch/pdf/assessment report/ar4/syr/ar4 syr spm.pdf.* Retrieved 10th August, 2014.

McCreary, R. (2009). Classroom management definition. *http://ehow.com/about 5438989 classroom management definition.html.* Retrieved 28th September, 2014.

Natural Resources Canada (2007).Climate change in Canada posters, *http://adaptation. nrcan.gc.ca/posters/cc_e.php*. Retrieved 15th September, 2014.

Oghuvbu, E. P. & Alakpo, T. E. (2008). Analysis of classroom management problems in primary schools in Delta State, Nigeria. *Contemporary Issues in Early Childhood* 9(4) 381-388.

Ojo, O., Ojo, K., & Oni, F. (2001). *Fundamental of physical and dynamic climatology.* Lagos: SEDEC Publishers.

Oleforo, N. A., Amaechi, N. V., & Nwachukwu, C. M. (2013). Environmental Security in the Management of Education in Nigeria. *A paper presented at the 32nd Annual Conference of Nigeria Association for Educational Administration and Planning. 8th – 10th October, 2013. Kwara State.*

Oleforo, N. A. (2014). *Educational Management in Nigeria: Theory and Practice.* Owerri: Cel-Bez Publishers.

Omotayo, A. M. (2010). *Agricultural Extension in the era of climate change, economic meltdown and food crises: Challenges and options.* Proceedings of the Obafemi Awolowo University, Ile-lfe Nigeria.

Onmigbodun, A. O. (2010). *Climate change and public health.* Paper presented at the 2nd Lagos State Summit on Global Climate Change at Eko Hotel and Suites Lagos. Nigeria. May 4 – 8.

Orukotan, A. & Oladipo, S. (1994*). Primary education in Nigeria.* Lagos: Nitax-Kuncho Publishers.

Tamuno, T. T. (2004*). Introduction to geography and environmental studies.* Port Harcourt: NSSI Books.

Tamuno, T. T. (2007). Climate change over the Niger Delta Region, Nigeria. Doctoral Seminar, University of Nigeria, Nsukka.

4

Domestication of School-based Management Policy as an Inclusive Approach to Addressing Educational Challenges in Nigeria: Implications

Princewill I. Egwuasi, *PhD* & Chiaka P. Denwigwe, *PhD*

Abstract

*T*his paper attempted to project the Domestication of School-Based Management Policy as a way of tackling educational challenges as well as promoting quality and access in education. It discussed School-based Management as a concept, citing the Australian experience, the roles and benefits of the SBMC, educational challenges and how to address them through domestication of SBMC, challenges to the success of SBMC and managing the development of SBMC. The Counselling implication was also discussed. It was concluded that the domestication of the SBM policy is a glaring opportunity to address the peculiar educational needs of communities in an attempt to take quality education down to the grassroots in Nigeria. A proper management of it was however suggested.

Key words: Domestication, Inclusive, Management

Introduction

Education at its best is expected to provide the foundation for life- long learning and also offer one the wherewithal to cope with the emerging trends and technologies. It should afford the learner the problem-solving skills that will turn him into a self-reliant individual; a quality that is indispensable in a fast-changing world. An attempt to match these ideals against the reality of the standard of education in Nigeria sends a chill down one's spine.

One is often tempted to conclude that there is a serious decline in the quality of formal education in Nigeria. Lovers of education decry the declining standard of education. According to Adegboye (2012), the standard of education in Nigeria today, is to say the least, at its lowest level. Reasons proffered for this decline in standard include among others lack of adequate teaching and learning materials, inability of government to implement educational policies appropriately, inability to properly train and retrain teachers, and so on.

Listing and debating the causes of decline in standard is not the solution to the malaise, rather a proactive suggestion on its amelioration is the best approach. This calls for a reform targeted at enabling the education sector in Nigeria to effectively accomplish its stated goals through adopting better structures, programmes and or practices that will replace existing ones.

Emphasis should be placed on strategies that would bring about improved quality and access in education, in addition to improving the financing and delivery of education services. A good way of doing this is to decentralise decision-making in education by introducing the School-Based Management concept (SBM). It was therefore as a result of an in-depth desire to add value to school governance through community participation that the idea of setting up school-Based Management Committees (SBMC) was bought in Nigeria.

The National Council on Education (NCE) in (2006) approved the establishment of SBMCs in all schools in the Federation, with the aim of decentralising the decision-making authority in order to carry along the stakeholders in the school community so as to enable schools to provide the needed social and economic benefits that portray the core values of their local environment. The SBMC initiative therefore, is to serve as a mechanism to enable stakeholders to participate actively in solving the problem of the basic education subsector.

In spite of the fact that the concept of SBM has been introduced in schools in the various states of Nigeria based on the national guidelines for implementation, the SBMCs have not been as functional as expected. This points out the obvious peculiarities in the various states, and calls for a need for the domestication of the SBMC policy as an inclusive approach to addressing educational challenges. The Universal Basic Education Commission (UBEC) is to fund the implementation of this policy while the Education Sector Support Programme in Nigeria (ESSPIN) of the UKAID provides the technical expertise and support.

The Concept of SBM

The SBM as a factor connecting the government, the school and its community has come a long way. Leithwood and Menza (1998) and Lewis (2006) opined that SBM is a way of decentralising decision-making authority to parents and communities so as to ensure that schools provide the social and economic benefits typical of the priorities and values of their local communities. Caldwell (2005) described it as the systematic decentralisation of authority and responsibility from the central government to the school level, to make decisions on significant matters related to school operations within a centrally-determined framework of goals, policies, curriculum, standards, and accountability. Mallen, Ogawe and Kranz (1990) viewed it as a formal alteration of governance structures, and as a form of decentralization that identifies the individual school as the primary unit of improvement. It relies on the redistribution of decision-making authority as the primary means through which improvement might be stimulated and sustained. By this the principals, teachers, parents, students and other members of the school community take up the responsibility for school operations and are in charge of decision-making while conforming to the standards/policies set by the central government. The SBM approach sees to it that the school becomes the key player in the business of educational improvement and ensures a reliance on the redistribution of the responsibilities as a major way of realising improvement in quality. In other words SBM entails a delegation of authority to manage and improve schools to principals, teachers, parents, and other stakeholders. The SBMC defines how the school funds made available to the schools by the government should be used and supplements them when necessary.

It then follows that one of the objectives of instituting an SBMC is to make for accountability and transparency in the way schools are managed. Thus Anderson (2005) asserted that school managers (members of the SBMC) must be accountable in three ways, namely:

- Accountable for adhering to rules and accountable to educational authorities
- Accountable for adhering to standards and accountable to their peers; and
- Accountable for student learning and accountable to the general public.

Ivbaze (2012) described SBM as a way of revitalizing the education sector towards making the schools child-friendly. It is a result-oriented avenue for key stake holders to effectively manage the schools. Emoabino (2012) cited by Ivbaze (2012) saw it as one of the strategies enunciated by government as a process in which all recognizable principal actors will participate genuinely in meeting the needs of schools and solving their problems.

SBMC - The Experiment in other Lands, Australia as a Case Study

Indonesia established a Commission of National Education in 2001 by following a law decentralizing education which was enacted in 1999. The Commission recommended the formation of school Councils at the school level to improve quality. On the basis of this, adopting of democratic principles and parental participation in school governance led to improvement of quality.

Werf, Creemers, and Guldenmond (2001) cited in Bandur (2008) revealed that involving parents in school councils led to significant improvement in the students' achievements. This empowerment of key stakeholders, through the forum of SBMC, led to efficient and effective schools with quality education by creating a healthier teaching/learning environment.

School-based Management has become a world-wide movement towards autonomy and share-decision making. Australia operates an education system that is constitutionally shared between states and territories. The result is a conflict in education systems with varying stages of developments in SBM. While the Australian Capital Territory (ACT) in 1967 had developed the concept of SBM with community participation similar to that in many countries (Gamage 2006, Gamage and Zajda 2005a), on the basis of an empirical survey, the ACT Department of Education and

Training (2004) reported an overall effectiveness of SBM, especially in decision-making at the school level and also in student outcomes. There was also improvement on learning environment.

On the other hand, the State of South Australia resolved in 1972 to enact the Education Act, recommending that school councils should be established in all state schools. By that Act, South Australia became the first state school system to establish school councils in the form of mandatory corporate bodies (Gamage, 2006). In the 2007 revision of the 1972 Act, the role of a school's governing council was set to include (1) broad directions, including school mission, vision, goals and a set of values that clearly focus on improving student learning; (2) developing broad directional policy statements to facilitate the achievement of the school vision and broad directions; (3) initiating and approving recommendations and strategies which conform with the policies set up by the systemic authorities; (4) monitoring progress including the expenditure of school budget and broad directives and school plans; (5) reporting progress that occurs with the principal and treasurer who provide data and timely reports that enable the governing council to confidently report to the Minister and community on how well the school is performing (South Australian Department of Education and Children's Services, 2008).

In Victoria, SBM commenced in 1975 with the enactment of the Education Act. It was reformed in 2006 to provide objectives, functions, power and authority to school Councils. The objectives for example are to (1) assist in the efficient governance of the school; (2) ensure that its decisions affecting students of the school are made having regards as a primary consideration to the best interest of the students at the school; and (3) enhance the educational opportunities of school (Victorian Education and Training Reform Act No. 24 /2006. Part 2.3, Division 3).

The Concept of Domestication

For the purpose of this paper, to domesticate the SBMC is to adopt the national guidelines in a way that they will be suitable to the peculiarities at the grass root levels. In other words, SBM policy should address the unique challenges of education at the grass roots.

Every state of the Federation including FCT for example has its unique challenges. This then calls for each state developing its own guidelines on SBMC rather than use the revised national guidelines. That is also to say that the contents of the national guidelines should not be swallowed hook, line and sinker but adjusted to suit the need of every state.

One should at this juncture, recall that the relocation of the seat of power from Lagos to Abuja caused civil servants, businessmen and other stakeholders to move into Abuja with their children and wards. Added to his is the centrality of the FCT which makes the influx of people very easy and so exerting more pressure on the existing school facilities. Obviously then there are competing needs that constantly weigh down education in the FCT. It is also worthy of mention that the public schools are assumed to be generally made for house helps and children of the low income group. This is another peculiarity for the FCT.

In the core north, the peculiar challenges are the issue of girl-child education and the almajiris while the concern in Anambra state is boy-child education. The menace by the militants is the challenge in the Niger delta areas while Imo and Abia states grapple with the challenge of kidnapping. The south west is not left out as it grapples with the problem of restive youths. All these peculiarities should be addressed through the domestication of the SBMC.

Members of the SBMC

Ivbaze (2012) suggested that the principal actors should include head teachers, parents/guardians, market women, administrators, community leaders, old boys/girls, civil organizations and artisans/professionals, etc. it should be noted that the Parent-teacher Association (PTA), being an organization of parents whose children or wards are in that particular school and the teachers of the school, is a part of the SBMC because one can be in the SBMC without his child necessarily being in the school. Thus the SBMC is an enlarged body which embraces the PTA. Guidance Counsellors have veritable roles to play for the success of the SBMC and so should be key members of the committee.

Roles/Benefits of SBM

The SBMC is capable of harnessing all necessary strategies to provide opportunities for community members to improve basic education delivery. The benefits accruable from SBM are numerous and are as follows:

- Effective monitoring of school operations
- Effective monitoring of school performance for example in the test scores and teacher attendance.
- Leading school improvement projects
- Tracking budgetary expenditures and helping to develop the school budget
- Raising of funds and creating endowment funds for the school
- Appointing and disciplining of teachers when necessary
- Providing template for the people to have input of both human and material resources for improved basic education (Ivbaze,2012)
- Ensuring regular payments of teachers' salaries (World Bank 1997)
- Ensuring that resources are distributed in a fair and transparent way (Caldwell,2005)
- Increasing transparency and thereby reducing corruption
- Empowering the managers at the school level to make decisions collectively
- Improving students' learning achievement and other outcomes through monitoring school personnel, improvement of students evaluation, ensuring

31

a closer match between school needs and policies and using resources more
efficiently

- Improving service delivery to the poor by increasing their choices and participation
in service delivery, by giving citizens a voice in school management, by making
information widely available and by strengthening the incentives for schools to
deliver effective services to the poor
- Providing avenue for community ownership of schools by providing tools
for community mobilization, even as it encourages sustainable educational
development and ensures accountability to school level (Ivbaze, 2012)
- Strengthening professional motivation
- Strengthening parental involvement in schools, etc.

Educational Challenges

The Nigerian educational system has over the years been ravaged by some challenges.
To tackle these challenges, it is needful to identify them. Such challenges include:

- Lack of needed capacity
- Insufficient government funding
- General economic poverty
- Non-implementation of educational policies
- Insufficient training and managerial capacity building
- Absenteeism and lateness to school among pupils and teachers
- Vandalization of school buildings by hoodlums
- Most pupils lack the basic rudiments hence according to Emeabino (2012) cited
in Ivbaze (2012), they cannot read and write nor can they identify the letters of
the alphabet.

Addressing Educational Challenges through Domestication of the SBM Policy

The Federal Government Policy on provision of basic education has been contributory
such that all tiers of government, communities and parents have specific roles to play
towards the provision of that education. According to Omorotionwan (2012) as cited
by Ivbaze (2012), the Federal Government through the Universal Basic Education
Commission (UBEC) and the State Universal Basic Education Board (SUBEB) has
taken the bull by the horn not only in sensitizing, mobilizing and paying advocacy
visits to schools/communities but has fashioned out policies, monitoring and evaluation
programmes, provided financial and material assistance for communities and schools
in Edo state by complementing the roles of the Governor. This can also be said of other
states of the federation. The state governments in turn complement the roles of the local
governments towards effective management of schools.

The idea of domestication of SBMC is to base it on the priorities of the state
government and in the aspiration of local communities for the improvement of education.

The ultimate goal of SBMC is the achievement of Education for all (EFA) and the Millennium Development Goals (MDGs) in Nigeria by 2020. It will ensure training and retraining of teachers to make them conversant with the modern teaching pedagogies and practices that will enable them address emerging challenges in education especially at the grass roots. SBMC will spur teachers to do the work, for which they are paid, eschew laziness, indolence and poor attitude to work.

The school head should not have fear of his job being threatened but should embrace the idea as a way of helping him perform better. He should view the SBMC as a constructively critical friend. SBMCs should be regarded as a channel through which government sets new pace for education through partnership.

In domesticating the SBM policy, the guidelines should be made practicable and tied to the needs/peculiarities of each community. This calls for the need for appropriate instruments for implementation. In other words, implementation is critical to the success of the programme. There should be more of monitoring of the implementation than talking about how and how not it should be done.

Also, the interest of the learner should be paramount, without any clash between the school authority and the SMBC.

Challenges to the Success of SBMC

Often times, many people in the communities in which the schools are located are not aware of the SBMCs and so do not contribute their quota to the school improvement plans. Perhaps if they were aware of their existence they would make efforts to make them functional. Since they were not aware, the needed critique they would have offered in order to uplift the schools has been lacking.

Where there is an awareness of the existence of SBMCs, enlightenment as to the nature and role of the SBMCs might be lacking. Also, not making the financial resources available at the school level may pose another problem. Ineffective governance structures at the state and local government leaving the communities with little or no capacity to contribute effectively is a problem. The limitation of the participation of community members in SBMC is a great challenge. The Education Sector Support Programme in Nigeria (ESSPIN) in its research report also highlighted the fact that the participation of women in SBMCs is highly constrained, especially in the northern states of Nigeria. The non-acceptance of children's participation was also highlighted. The lack of clarity in the role of the Local Government Education Authorities (LGEAs) in supplying materials to SBMCs was also noted.

Managing the Development of SBMCs

As a fairly new concept in Nigeria, albeit it has worked very successfully in countries like Australia and New Zealand among others, the effective actualization of the SBM policy requires that a process be put in place for managing its development.

To that effect, the national guidelines gave a step-by-step procedure on its adaptation and adoption for implementation in the states.

These Procedures include:

- Documentation, which entails each state and the FCT deriving its own policy document from the national guidelines to suit its purposes.
- Establishment of state Task Teams (STTs) to drive the implementation. The STT is appointed by the state's commissioner for education and must include social mobilization support staff and representatives of PTAs, Local Education Authorities (LEAs), Non-governmental Organizations (NGOs), Civil Society organizations (CSOs) and Faith-based organizations (FBOs).
- Capacity development, which entails training of master trainers who, in turn, train the other levels of the implementation process, including the SBMC members themselves.
- On-going capacity development to ensure follow-up mentoring, monitoring and evaluation as well as reporting of outcome**s.**

Implications to Counselling

To achieve the main objectives of the SBM policy, school managers (members of the SBMC) as opined by Anderson (2005) must be accountable in three ways, namely:

- Accountable for adhering to rules and accountable to educational authorities
- Accountable for adhering to standards and accountable to their peers; and
- Accountable for student learning and accountable to the general public.

This implies that counselling is needed to provide an array of specialized programmes or activities which would encourage wise choices and decisions that would culminate in accountability as expected. This will eventually rub off on the learners who are the major beneficiaries of quality education. Prominent among the roles of counselling in driving the SBM policy is its indispensable role in advocating for an enriched curriculum geared towards the individual and societal needs. Counselling will go a long way in helping the SBMC to meet the target of addressing the problems emanating from the peculiarities of communities such as gender issues, the issue of the Almajiris, restive youths, menace by militants and kidnapping, etc., as already stated. It also implies that to drive the domestication of the SBM vision, counselling is needed in advocating for training and retraining of teachers, provision of needed teaching and learning materials and making necessary funds available.

Conclusion

The domestication of the SBM policy is a welcome approach for addressing educational challenges. If properly driven, it will go a long way to ensure the realization of the ideals of education. The experiences of countries like Australia in which it has successfully worked buttress the fact that it is a worthy venture. The domestication of the SBM policy stands out clearly as an opportunity to address the peculiar educational needs of communities in an attempt to take quality education down to the grassroots.

References

Adegboye, D. (2012). *Occupy till I come: The Practical Aspects of Contending for the Faith.* A Paper Presented at the 2012 Divine Commonwealth Conference (DIVCCON) at the Ecumenical Centre Abuja, Nigeria. P2.

Anderson, J. A. (2005). Accountability in Education. *Education Policy Series.* The International Institute for Educational Planning and the International Academy of Education; Paris and Brussels.

Bandur, A. (2008). A Study of the Implementation of School –Based Management in Flores Primary Schools in Indonesia. (An Unpublished Ph.D Thesis. The University of Newcastle, Australia. *www. Wikipedia. Com*

Caldwell, B. (2005). School-based Management Education Policy Booklet series 3. International Institute for Educational Planning-UNESCO: *http://www.iaoed.org/files/Edpol3.pdf.*

Emoabino, S. (2012), cited by Ivbaze O., (2012). Domestication of School-based Management Committee in Edo. Nigeria Observer Online Edition, Sept 6. 2012. *www.nigerianobservernews.com/180220.*

Education Sector Support Programme in Nigeria, 423 SBMC Development Progress Report, 2012. *Report of Qualitative Research in Five States of Nigeria.*

Gamage, D.T & zajda, J. (2005a). Decentralization and school-Based Management : A Comparative Study of Self-governing Schools Model. *Educational Practice and Theory.27(2) 35-38.*

Gamage, D.T (2006a).Effective Participatory School Administration, Leadership, and Management: Does it affect the trust levels of stakeholdes? *National Council of Professors of Educational Administration, 1(2)1-17.*

Ivbaze, O, (2012). Domestication of SBMC in Edo, Nigeria Observer online edition Sept. 6, 2012. *www.nigeriaobservernews.om/180220.*

Leithwood, K. & Menza, T. (1998). Forms and Effects of School-based Management: A Review. *Educational policy* 12(3):325

Lewis, M (2006). *Decentralising Education: Do Communities and Parents Matter?"* Mimeo Centre for Global Development, Washington, D. C.

Mallen, B., Ogawe, R. T. and Kranz, J. (1990). What do we know about Site-based Management: a Case Study of the Literature- A call for Research. In *Choice and Control in American Education,* Vol 2, 289-342, ed. W. H. Clune & J. F. Witte. London: Falmer Press.

Omorotionwan, E. (2012), in Ivbaze (2012). Domestication of SBMC in Edo, Nigeria Observer online edition Sept. 6, 2012. *www.nigerianobservernews.com/180220*.

Samuel, E. B., Meriem, G., Priyam, S.& Juontel, W. (2012). Transparency in Primary Schools. Enhancing School Management in Ghana. *Report for Transparency International Workshop in Development Practice.*

Werf, G., Greemers, B., Guldenmond, H. (2001). Improving Parental Involvement in Primary Education in Indonesia: Implementation,Effects and Costs. *School Effectiveness* and School Improvement, 12(14).

Wohlsletter & Mohrman, S. (1993). School-based Management Strategies for Success. *http://www2.ed.gov/pn....*

World Bank (1997). *World Development Report: The state in a Changing World.* New York: oxford university press for the World Bank.

CURRICULUM ISSUES

5

K To 12 Basic Education Program: Basic Features and Implications to HEI's

Flora V. Javier, *Ed.D*

Introduction

Many seminars and conferences on K to 12 have been conducted in various parts of the country to inform the community about the changes that will inevitably take place with the implementation of the K to 12 Enhanced Education Reform Agenda. This paper will present highlights of these conferences with the objective of elucidating the readers on what changes we should expect, especially in private higher educational institutions, with the full implementation of the program.

The need to reform the present educational system of the Philippines is not a new idea. As early as 1925, studies have observed the inadequacies of basic education. This was shown by the findings of the Monroe Survey in 1925 and the Presidential Task Force on Education in 2008 which recommended among others, the adding or restoring of Grade 7 or adding an extra year to basic education. (Piamonte, 2012). This was also was underscored in the 2011 Global Competitiveness Report from the World Economic Forum which showed among others that except for Cambodia, the Philippines continues to lag behind all ASEAN countries with the ranking of 75th out of 142 countries, and out of 8 ASEAN countries, firth in Quality of Education and eight or last in Quality of Science and Math Education and Capacity for Innovation (Angara, 2012;Quijano, 2012;Ferrer, 2012)

Educators and legislators have highlighted in their speeches that the Philippines is one of the only three countries in the world which has a 10-year pre- university program which disadvantages our high school graduates in terms of admission to international universities and/or recognition of professionals. The Washington Accord prescribes 12 year of primary education for engineering graduate before they can be recognized as engineering professionals. The European Union's Bologna Accord similarly requires 12 years of basic education for students applying for graduate school or professional practice. The Association of Southeast Asian Nations (ASEAN) is also moving toward an ASEAN Economic Community (AEC) by 2015. In just three year's time Senator Angara said we will be one regional market where there will be free movement of skilled labor as well as goods and capital and if our educational system remains in the status quo, we will appear like a sore thumb in Southeast Asia being the only country with a 10-year basic education cycle (Cruz, 2012, Angara, 2012).

The foregoing sad realities point to the urgent need for a massive transformation of the basic education system. To respond to this monumental challenge, President

Aquino laid the 10-point agenda for basic education topped by the 12 year global education standards. The 10 Reform Initiatives in Basic Education aims to enable schools to respond adequately to local needs while allowing its graduates to explore and maximize opportunities beyond the Philippine shores. These initiatives are listed as follows: 1) 12-year basic education cycle; 2) Universal pre-schooling for all; 3) Madaris Education as a sub-system in the current education system; 4) Technical and vocational education as an alternative stream in senior high school; 5) Every child a reader by Grade I; 6) Science and Mathematics Proficiency 7) Expand government assistance to private education; 8) Use of mother tongue-based multilingual education; 9) Quality textbooks; and 10) Covenant with LGU's to build more schools (Aquino, 2012, Luistro,2012).

What is K to 12?

It is a system of basic education wherein Filipino children aged 4 to 19 will undergo free public school system and receive the following diplomas in their graduation ceremonies: elementary (after Grade 6), junior high (after Grade 10) and senior high (after Grade 12). Entry to any Tertiary Level education will require a senior high school diploma. Private schools may hold graduation ceremonies after Pre School or Kindergarten.(Cruz, 2012)

K to 12 builds on the reform thrusts of the Basic Education Sector Reform Agenda that began in 2006 which is aimed at improving access and quality of basic education in the country through the 5 key reform thrusts (KRT) namely: (KRT1) standard-driven management or continuous school improvement; (KRT2) teacher education and development; (KRT3) national learning strategies that produce the desired learning outcomes which K to 12 as the flagship strategy; (KRT4) quality assurance and accountability and (KRT5) organizational development.

K to 12 is not the program of the Department of Education alone. It is a joint program of the three educational agencies, namely Dep Ed, CHED & TESDA in concert with the students, parents, teachers and administrators from public and private schools, education experts, government agencies and legislature, HEI's, business sectors and civil society organizations. As stated in the Philippine Development Plan 2011-2016, with the K to 12 program, the basic education curriculum will be transformed so that it will produce holistically developed learners who possess the 21st century skills and are prepared for higher education, middle level skill development, employment and entrepreneurship. In the words of Education Secretary Armin Luistro (2012), the K to 12 program is one concrete response to reverse the steady decline and to move towards its goal of long term education reform (Quijano, 2012;Ferrer,2012).

The Basic Education Reform Agenda provides that all public and private schools must adhere to the minimum standards prescribed in the K to 12 Basic Education program which include among others: a) age requirement, i.e students begin elementary at age 6 after at least one year in Kindergarten; b) students go through at least one year of Kindergarten and 12 years of basic education; c) curriculum – Kinder and

Basic Education program offered by all schools must have the contents specified in K to 12 Basic Education curriculum. However private schools have the leeway to offer innovative courses beyond the prescribed curricula. The K to 12 Basic Education curriculum will be enhanced characterized by the following: 1) it is learner-centered and focuses on the optimum development of the Filipinos; 2) It is decongested to allow for mastery of competencies; 3) It is seamless, meaning the content, content and performance standards and competencies are in a continuous and will follow the spiral progressive model; 4) It is responsive and flexible to answer the local needs; 5) It is enriched, i.e. the curriculum is integrative, inquiry-based, constructivists and technology enhanced. The other features include Mother tongue as a learning area and medium of instruction (Luistro,2012).

As planned, the implementation of K to 12 will be phased and gradual to minimize disruptions. Universal Kindergarten was implemented in 2011-2012. The enhanced K to 12 curriculum will be progressively implemented starting from Grade 1 and Grade 7 (HS Yr 1) in 2012-2013. The new curriculum for the succeeding Grade levels will be progressively introduced from 2013 to 2016 with the first cohort of students entering Grade 11 in the 2016 and then Grade 12 in 2017. The students who entered Grade 7 in June 2012 will be the first batch of graduates with Senior high school diploma during the SY 2017-2018. The Grade I students in 2012-2013will be the first batch to undergo the full K to 12 Basic Education program who will graduate during the SY 2023-2024 (Quijano, 2012;Ferrer,2012).

Implications to HEI's

Private HEI's may handle the Senior High School (Grade 12) to solve the problem of the gap which will result from lack of college freshmen enrollees in 2016 and 2017, which is expected to roll over until the first batch of Grade 12 graduates get to fourth year if they enroll in a four year college course or longer if they choose a course that requires 5 0r 6 yrs or more (ex. Engineering, Dentistry, Medicine). But students who will enroll in Grades 11 & 12 will not be called College students because they are in fact still high school students. The teachers who will teach them therefore should have licenses or be LET passers. Cruz (2012) said most of the subjects in the proposed Senior High School curriculum will come from the college General Education Curriculum.

The other concern is the salary scale of teachers. Most college teachers are paid by hour; most high school teachers are paid monthly based on prevailing rates among high schools and on the school's resources. HEI's college teachers will therefore have to do a financial sacrifice. Cruz (2012) also said that DepEd may lease the facilities of HEI's for Senior High School classes, giving the HEI's income. However, even if DepEd leases the facilities but utilizes their own teachers that leaves the General Education teachers with no loads. If DepEd leases and the HEI's facilities and allows the HEI to field its own college teachers to teach the Senior High School. HEI's will settle for lower pay for their college teachers.

There are other issues and concerns related to the K to 12 program which concerned agencies are still discussing such as revision of the college curriculum and the subsequent shortening of most 4-year courses to 3 years because of the removal of the General Education subjects. We will await all these changes. Meanwhile HEI's should prepare its General Education teachers by offering education subjects or the Teacher Certificate Program (TCP) to enable them to take LET and be qualified to teach in high school.

As a concluding statement, I believe that the success of the K to 12 Basic Education program will depend on the concerted efforts, support and openness of all education stakeholders from the government and the private sectors. Surely, it will require a lot of budget and teacher training.It will also need a paradigm shift especially for HEI's which will feel the greatest impact next to parents perhaps, as the program progresses in its implementation. As we educators find ourselves at the crossroad, we are enjoined by no less than our President Benigno Aquino III to give this program a chance. Let's all welcome the changes and pray that the K to 12 program as well as the other education initiatives of the government will truly bring the much needed reform in the Philippine educational system.

References

Angara, E. J. (2012). *Legislative Agenda on Education Reform,* 4th National COCOPEA Congress, UST Manila

Aquino, B. S. (2012). *Reforming Philippine Education: Issues, Challenges and Solutions.* Keynote Speech, 4th National COCOPEA Congress, University of Santo Tomas

Cruz, I.. *Philippine Star.* January 5, 2012, January 12, 2012, January 19, 2012 and January 26, 2012, February 2, 2012

Estrada, N. J. (2012). *Legislative Updates, Post COCOPEA Conference.* St. Michael's College, Laguna

Ferrer, R. (2012). *K to 12 Education Program, Post COCOPEA Conference.* St. Michael's College, Laguna

Luistro, A. A. (Bro). (2012). FSC. 4th National COCOPEA Congress, University of Sto. Thomas, Manila

Luistro, A. (2007). *The K to 12 Curriculum our First Step to Recovery PDI*

Piamonte, M. U. (2012). Jr. *Legislative Agenda on Education Reforms in the 15th Congress,* 4th National COCOPEA Congress, UST Manila

Dr. Princewill Egwuasi

Quijano, Y. (2012). *K to 12 Education Program, Post COCOPEA Conference,* St. Michael's College, Laguna

Tenedero, H. S. (2012). *K to 12 Curriculum and Its Stakeholders.* Manila Bulletin

Teves, G., Nilo A. S.; Valero C. (2011). *K to 12 in Focus.* Educators Magazine for Teachers

6

Curriculum Issues in Nigeria

Inua Magaji

Introduction

Education is an instrument of change for national development. It is a social process and the medium for the acquisition of relevant knowledge, skills and attitudes for survival in a changing world. The strengthening of democratic institutions witnessed world over including Nigeria and the rapid increase in globalization have become more prominent in the 21st century. Nations desire closer cooperation, improvement in the quality of life, respect for the rule of law and Human Rights and peaceful co-existence among communities and nations.

In responding to these issues, Nigeria has been part of the global deliberations on Education for All (EFA), which have been reflected in the national education policies and programmes. Notable among these policies are the National Economic Empowerment and Development Strategies (NEEDS) developed, adopted and implemented in 2004. NEEDS has four critical elements which are: value re-orientation, poverty eradication, wealth generation and job creation.

NEEDS is also anchored on the Millennium Development Goals (MDGS). Since education is the vehicle for cultural transmission and economic transformation, basic education must transform and empower people. Hence, the relevance of education in the actualization of NEEDS cannot be overemphasized. Thus, if education is the vehicle for achieving the goals of NEEDS, its contents and processes of delivery should be reformed in the context of improving the quality of life and facilitating the cherished global values earlier mentioned. One of the policies that were adopted to achieve this lofty objective was the vision 2020.

The rapid increase in globalisation and the strengthening of democratic institutions has become more pronounced in the 21st century. As nations sought closer cooperation, the improvement of basic life quality and learning to live together became more critical. Respect for the rule of law, basic human rights, improvement of the environment, peaceful coexistence across nationalities and communities, reduction of poverty, combating HIV/AIDS pandemic and economic restructuring are some of the global issues that transcends national boundaries. Nigeria's response to these global emerging issues was the adoption of vision 2020.

The first Pillar of the Vision 2020 is to guarantee the well-being and productivity of the people with education as the bedrock. This will lead to establishment of a modern and vibrant education system that ensures the maximum development of the potentials of individuals and promotes a knowledge-driven society that propels the nation's development. The ability to acquire and utilize knowledge and skills effectively is the key to the growth and development that will propel Nigeria to become one of the 20 largest economies by the year 2020.

A modern and vibrant education system entails wide–ranging activities that would ensure functional and qualitative education of the highest possible standards at basic, post-basic and tertiary levels. The primary goals of achieving this include providing access to quality education at all levels, improved learning and teaching infrastructure, according greater importance to science, information technology, technical, vocational education and training. Thus, if education will be used to achieve the acquisition of knowledge, then its contents and delivery processes should be reformed in the context of improving the quality of life and facilitating the peaceful co-existence of the people of Nigeria and the world at large. Curriculum reformation is therefore needed to achieve this lofty objective. What then is curriculum?

Curriculum is a formal academic plan for the learning experiences of students in pursuit of knowledge. The term curriculum, broadly defined, includes goals for student learning (skills, knowledge and attitudes); content (the subject matter in which learning experiences are embedded); sequence (the order in which concepts are presented); learners; instructional methods and activities; instructional resources (materials and settings); evaluation (methods used to assess student learning as a result of these experiences); and adjustments to teaching and learning processes, based on experience and evaluation. Although the term curriculum is variably used, this definition is sufficiently inclusive and dynamic to accommodate for the many innovations that involve instructional methods, sequencing, and assessments as well as instructional goals and content, all of which have been implemented in order to improve learning.

Forces for Change

According to Afe (2013), curricular taught in Nigerian schools today at all levels are outdated. While there have been several attempts at curriculum reforms at all levels, none of these have been successful in lifting the education fortunes of the country. While it was desirable to reform the colonial curriculum as the country progressed, the ones that replaced them have not been as successful as that of the colonial system, partly because they were not designed to be in touch with current realities of the Nigerian society. For example, while Nigeria needs graduates who are self-reliant and who can take initiatives in globally competitive crafts and inventions, what we have is a situation where graduates from primary, secondary and tertiary institutions in the country graduate without having an iota of idea on how what they learnt in school will apply in practical life. Unfortunately, the reality is that in most cases, they are not applicable.

The desire for change in the educational curriculum is not primarily a function of how old the curriculum has lasted, but how fast the society and its needs are changing, especially in response to the matrix of internal and global competitiveness. In this information age, the world is changing faster than ever before. While not all aspects of a curriculum change at the same pace and at the same time, the aspects that change are usually so significant that only a constant review of the curriculum can guarantee functional education of the students. In many countries, general curriculum review takes place every five years while individual changes may take place because of new research breakthrough or major economic, political or social changes but not in Nigeria. A careful examination of the educational curriculum in Nigeria at all levels will reveal that much emphasis is still placed on the doctrinal and philosophical bases of the subjects studied by the students. There is very little or no emphases on application skills that ensure that what a student learns remain relevant in his life after school. It is not enough to have a curriculum that is in touch with developmental realities of a country or even the global world. A fundamental issue here is that the curriculum must contain practical skills that guarantee self-reliance by those who studied subjects. Educational institutions all over the world are shifting from delivery of doctrinal curriculum to a balanced delivery of doctrines and skills, with more emphasis on those cross-disciplinary skills that will still be relevant in life whether a person practices the trade he learnt in school or not. Contrary to this, academic discourses in Nigeria are seen as classroom discourses while the graduate is left on his own to figure out how best to make use of the information he learnt in school.

In an article published in one of the editions of Business Day Newspaper in 2012, the author lamented how, on two different occasions, two professors consulted by his company as experts in their fields could not deliver on the jobs and returned several millions of naira they had been paid after about six months of doing nothing. It dawned on the company that the professors were merely academic experts who contented themselves with the doctrinal issues on the subjects they claimed expertise in and published several papers, without knowing anything about how they will apply in practice. How then can these professors produce relevant graduates who are employable after graduation? This is not the case in countries that have functional education system.

The high cost of doing business in Nigeria and the near-comatose state of infrastructure in the country also negatively impacts on the curriculum taught in Nigeria's educational institutions. Nigeria is highly a consumerist nation and the few industries in the country seem to have lost confidence in the products of Nigeria's educational systems and would rather prefer products from foreign institutions. In countries where things work, curriculum designs and reviews are carried out based on current or future industry needs. When companies encounter serious challenges in their operations, they refer them to education and research institutions who in turn design curriculums that can help in tackling those problems, devise new ways of doing things or pursue new research breakthroughs that will improve quality of lives and enhance competitiveness in the industries. This is why companies finance research initiatives and grant scholarships in their areas of interest in developed countries. Unfortunately, this is not the case in Nigeria. Even the few multi-national corporations that award scholarships to Nigerian students do so as a matter of community service or corporate social responsibility and not because they are expecting any meaningful return from their investments. Before there can be functional curriculum in Nigeria's educational system, this broken synergy between the institutions and the industries must be fixed.

What Should Be Done

Education in the generic and global context has been identified as a strategic instrument for social and economic transformation. NEEDS has recognized that for the culture of reform to be sustained, education should be used to empower the people.

The difference between developed and developing countries is not found in:

Abundance of natural resources; for if it were, Japan will have been very poor and Nigeria very rich. Contrary, Japan with virtually no natural resources is the second economy of the world, while countries such as Gabon and Nigeria are debt ridden.

Age of the country: It is known that Egypt as the oldest civilization of the world is poor country, while the economies of emerging countries such as Taiwan, Singapore, Malaysia etc. are developing at a very fast rate.

Agricultural endowment: Even though virtually nothing grows in Switzerland, it is the "safe" of the world with a strong and vibrant economy.

The difference can be found in respect for the rule of law, strict protection of human rights, positive value orientation, strategic knowledge management and good governance. Rich countries strive to not only acquire and sustain these values and virtues but systematically use education to bring these about. Rich countries devote most of their resources to educational development and continually restructure their school curriculum at all levels to facilitate people empowerment through education. Nigeria and other developing countries could join the bandwagon by taking the following measures:

- **Adoption of Computer Education Curriculum**

The Nigerian Educational Research and Development Council (NERDC) with a mandate in curriculum development should develop curriculum with emphasis on creative thinking, entrepreneurial skills, positive social and cultural values. Adoption of this form of education will result to;
  - Development of reasonable level of competence in ICT applications that will propel entrepreneurial skills
  - Promotion of technology literacy by incorporating technology skills in learning
  - Improvement of knowledge that would solve complex, real-world problems
  - Production of students with technology literacy, workforce, and academic skills necessary to compete in a global environment;

- Job creation and self reliance

- **Teachers Understanding of the Philosophy and Objectives of Curriculum**

Odubunmi observed that a teacher who does not understand the philosophy of a subject might find it difficult to teach the subject. This is a truism with respect to subject teaching. Also, the objectives provide the direction for implementation of the curriculum. Hence, it is pertinent to ensure that teachers understand the teaching requirement in the attainment of curriculum objectives. Furthermore, it is not a new phenomenon that a large number of school teachers demonstrate ignorance of the objectives of curriculum.

- **Capacity Building**

The quality of teachers is a determinant of the quality of the educational system. Teachers constitute the human resource required for the facilitation of achievement of the objectives of curriculum and its implementation. Since what teachers do in the classrooms and laboratories are largely dependent on what they know. Capacity building for teachers is imperative for the implementation of curriculum.

The training and retraining of teachers is necessary for them to enact reform-based curriculum. The capacity building process should be systematic and continuous through science workshops, seminars, enlightenment programmes on the reform, orientation courses and other useful educative activities.

This is because teachers themselves like the pupils and students require support to be effective in the delivery of the curriculum. Furthermore, curriculum materials such as teachers' guides, handbooks and manuals should be designed to improve teacher quality as one potential vehicle towards supporting them.

Professional growth and development during service should be encouraged. The number of qualified teachers presently in the schools is grossly inadequate for the Basic Education Curriculum. Nigerian teachers are ill-motivated and often of low morale. Teachers at all levels at one time have embarked on strike for improved salary. The recruitment of teachers cannot be overlooked especially in the new subject areas.

- **Quality of Curriculum Delivery**

The spiral curriculum requires child-centered and activity-oriented teaching/ learning process. The use of different teaching methods and strategies to ensure students understanding of topics has become imperative. The guided discovery method of teaching which is encouraged in science teaching is time-consuming and requires planning and dedication on the part of the teacher. It is interesting to note that classroom activities which most teachers perceive as indicative of good teaching are still predominantly teacher-centred activities. New teaching techniques and strategies that are highly learner-centred such as concept mapping and cooperative learning should be taught to teachers during capacity building. Process-base learning requires the utilization of instructional materials and other teaching apparatus in this new dispensation. Most importantly, students' participation must be prominent in the methodology. New techniques such as concept mapping and cooperative learning should be taught to teachers to improve their teaching competencies. Effects of concept mapping technique on the performance of students in science subjects have been widely researched and documented empirically (Okebukola 1997; Adebanjo 2007. A cooperative learning technique is yet another that has the potentiality to bring about meaningful learning (Okebukola 1997). There should be good presentation of relevant information by the teacher and the encouragement of interaction among pupils and students. Also, curricular and experiential knowledge possessed by the teacher with adequate display of such knowledge through involving students will result in meaningful learning.

- **Production and Provision of Textbooks and Other Instructional Materials**

The information in the UBEC 2006 document is that free textbooks will be provided for four core subjects in primary schools and five core subjects in Junior Secondary Schools. These include Basic Science and Technology, Basic Science and Basic Technology in Basic 1-6 and Basic 7-9, respectively. The need for the provision of textual materials for pupils and students cannot be ignored. Many pupils and students come to school without books for a number of reasons, one of which is poverty. The production and provision of textual and other instructional materials should be a priority for quality delivery of the curriculum. Simple science apparatus and equipment should be part of the package in the provision of Government in the Basic Science and Technology component of UBE Programme. It could be argued that teachers at these levels should improvise instructional materials. There is a limit to the extent of improvisation realizing that some equipment cannot be improvised. Besides, teachers and students require exposure and practical experience with standard and modern apparatus and equipment.

- **Enrolment and Class Size**

It should be expected that since the UBE is to be free and compulsory, the enrolment figure is bound to increase and result in large classes. Presently, the average class size is larger than what is stipulated in the National Policy on Education (Federal Republic of Nigeria, 2004). Large classes would hinder curriculum implementation because the quality of teaching will be poor due to inadequate teacher: student ratio. In addition, data on number of eligible children for the UBE is desirable. This will assist in determining the likely enrolment figure of pupils and students at the Lower, Middle and Upper Basic levels of the programme. The class size also has implication for the quality of teaching, assessment, use of instructional materials and ultimately quality of learning.

- ## Mode of Assessment and Conduct of Examination

The UBE policy indicates that major mode of assessment will be school based or Continuous Assessment (CA) of learning outcome under the UBE programme to determine the child's progress from one level to the other. In addition, a Continuous Assessment Instrument has been standardized and would be applied nationwide. The proposed instrument has to be available to all schools at the correct time for uniformity and objectivity of assessment without which the CA of different quality will result in serious disparity in the assessment of learning outcome in different schools. All forms of evaluation: diagnostic, formative, illuminative and summative should be utilized in the assessment procedures. Assessment should not be limited to the cognitive domain alone because science leads to acquisition of various skills, the affective and psychomotor domains too should be assessed. Thus, the mode of assessment and conduct of examination must be effective and uncompromised in the successful implementation of the curriculum.

- ## Monitoring, Supervision, Inspection and Evaluation

Supervision and Inspection are viewed as instruments of administration that affect the achievement of the objectives of an educational programme. Supervisory duties directly affect the curriculum which is the academic programme of the school hence the quality of instruction. Supervisory duties which rest on the school head or principal should be given the utmost attention. Several measures should be put in place to ensure thorough supervision of the proper use of the approved syllabus, scheme and record of work, the lesson plan, the time table and school laboratory.

- ## Infrastructural Facilities

The disarticulation of JSS from SSS in order to ensure the existence of two separate administrations in the existing secondary schools would not only require more qualified teachers, it would also entail the provision of additional infrastructures in the junior secondary school. There is the need for new laboratories especially if students had been sharing laboratories with the senior secondary school students. This would enable the exposure of J.S. (Basic 7-9) Students to practical laboratory experiences, acquisition of science process skills, scientific attitudes in their Basic Science and Technology subjects without any hindrance.

Conclusions

Addressing the issues discussed above is a serious challenge to all the stakeholders of education in this country because of the syndrome of Nigerian factor. Problems with previous education program such as the lack of political will, inadequate funding, insufficient quantity and quality of teachers in all fields should not be allowed to derail functional programs proposed above. The lack of adequate data to work with, lack of proper records and lack of managerial capacity should be tackled with utmost sincerity of purpose. The cooperation among the federal and state governments, UBEC, SUBEB, NTI, NERDC, Universities, Schools, Teachers, Parents and other curriculum implementation agencies is imperative for implementation, functionality and sustainability of curriculum content in Nigeria.

Recommendations

- Government should embark on massive continuous orientation and training/ programmes for in-service teachers towards the implementation of the UBE curriculum.
- Government should ensure a survey of infrastructural facilities in the public schools and commence the process of renovation and building of new structures with immediate effect.
- Government should make copies of the New Basic Education curriculum available to primary and junior secondary schools to ensure adequate implementation of the curriculum.
- Government should ensure that the NERDC produces adequate number of textbooks for students, teachers' guides and manuals for the schools
- Class size should be streamlined to correspond with the provision in the National Policy on Education for effective teaching.
- The supervisory and inspectorate units of Ministries of Education should be empowered with adequate human and material resources to constantly inspect schools and ensure that curriculum delivery is adequate
- Government and schools should encourage and support teachers membership of professional bodies such as Science Teachers' Association of Nigeria (STAN)
- There is need to incorporate Information, Communication Technology (ICT) into capacity building in the Sciences and Teachers Education programmes in Nigeria
- The Teachers' Registration Council should be responsible for the regulation standard and practice in the teaching profession.
- Funding of research into different aspects of the Universal Basic Education curriculum has become desirable and imperative.

References

Afe, B. (2006). The Dwindling Standard of Education in Nigeria: The way Forward, Guest Lecture presented at Lead City University, Ibadan.

Okebukola, P. (1997). Old, New and Current Technology in Education. *UNESCO Africa, 14* (15), 7-18.

Adebanjo A, A. (2007). Effect of Instructional Media on the Learning of Computer in Junior Secondary Schools. *African Research Journal of Educational Research Vol. II No 1 & 2. Pp 71-75.*

Federal Republic of Nigeria (2004). *National Policy on Education.* 4th ed. Lagos: Nigerian Educational Research and Development Council.

7

Organization of Teaching Practice in Colleges of Education in Nigeria

Prof. Jane I. Alamina & Samuel Jeremiah *PhD*

Introduction

Teaching practice is a major component of the teacher education preparatory programme both at the pre-service and in-service sub-sector. It can be compared to the Housemanship, Law school and Industrial training programmes of such professions as Medicine, Law and Engineering to mention but a few. Teaching practice programme should be seen as a cardinal curriculum package as it provides avenue to access the quality and credibility of teacher's entry point into the teaching profession. The implication of this is that, it is through teaching practice exercise that the student teachers are trained to acquire the professional skills of a trained teacher. Such skills may include pedagogical skills, classroom management, uses and application of instructional materials, knowledge of school records, evaluation strategies, knowledge of the learner relative to their individual differences and even school and community relationship. These issues and others not stated here are very vital skills to be displayed by student teachers on teaching practice.

The effectiveness of teaching practice on teacher training institutions and more specifically Colleges of Education depends basically on how it is organized or planned towards the achievement of its goals. Hence, this chapter examines among others the concept and objectives of teaching practice, procedures for the organization of teaching practice and the roles of various stakeholders in the organization of teaching practice. These major headings will provide the reader a better understanding in the explanation of the major topic.

Meaning and Objectives of Teaching Practice

Teaching practice commonly called T.P. is a practical aspect or component of teacher professional training. Michael (2009) explained that teaching practice provides the appropriate classroom environment for the transformation of theories of teaching into practical experience. Joke (2010) noted that teaching practice is an opportunity given to student teacher to put into practice the various educational theories they have studied. Such education theories emerged from the various educational courses they have studied prior to the period of the teaching practice exercise. In the Nigeria Certificate in Education (NCE) minimum standard for such theoretical courses include EDU 112 (Educational Psychology), EDU 113 (Principles and Methods of Teaching), EDU 124

(Theory and Practice of Child Friendly Schools), EDU 211 (Practicum in Classroom Management), EDU 212 (Educational Technology), EDU 213 (Micro Teaching Theory), EDU 222 (Curriculum Studies I) and EDU 223 (Micro Teaching Practicum) FRN (2012). It is important to note that the content areas of these courses are organized to prepare the student teacher for the teaching practice exercise. This accounts for the reason why teaching practice in Colleges of Education in Nigeria (based on the new minimum standard) is now a six months exercise carried out immediately after the second year of the three years programme.

Vipene and Jeremiah (2012) noted that teaching practice is an opportunity given to student teachers to gain practical classroom experience under the supervision of an expert or experts. The practical experience according this definition relates to the various teaching skills to be demonstrated by the student teacher. The application of such skills must be assessed by a trained teacher or supervisor who is believed to be more knowledgeable than the student teacher.

This observation tend to agree with Jeremiah (2013), explaining that teaching practice is a period which provide opportunities under typical school condition in selected co-operating schools for student teachers to secure experiences in observing and participating actively in diverse educational activities of teachers in school. The major point of agreement in the above analysis of teaching practice exercise is that the student teachers are supervised and evaluated with the view of gaining practical experience in classroom management, uses of instructional materials, applications of good teaching methods, uses of school records, practical code of conduct and proper teacher pupils relationship. Thus it is teaching practice exercise that distinguishes between a student teacher and those of other profession.

Philosophy of Teaching Practice

The philosophy that underlines the teaching practice exercise is articulated by the National Teachers Institute (2002) as follows:

- To provide adequate field experience for the professional development of teachers;
- To provide opportunities for Student-Teachers to engage in a professional exercise in observing, sharing, participating in school activities and practical teaching;
- To serve as a means of assessing the professional competence of student teachers; and
- To provide student trainees opportunities for translating theory into practice.

General Objectives of Teaching Practice

Teaching practice exercise is expected to enable the student attain the following objectives:

- Gain practical experience in academic, professional, social, physical and curricular related to teaching as a profession;
- Acquire adequate wealth of practical experiences from all staff they are likely to be in contact with through active participation in school activities;
- Gain valuable insights for use as needed, through school and classroom observation and analysis;
- Bring the student teacher in direct contact with such significant issues as the functions and responsibilities of various categories of school staff, academic and non-academic;
- Observe at first hand, the different features of school curriculum at work, i.e. the official and actual curriculum, core curriculum and how each contributes to learning;
- Become familiar with school records and the complex set of rules, relations and records of all kinds that all teachers should know;
- Learn to work in close collaboration with an experienced cooperating teacher who is willing to share his/her experiences with the student teachers;
- Develop competence in proper lesson preparation, delivery and assessment;
- Acquire those valuable personality attributes associated with outstanding teachers e.g. warmth, empathy and tolerance;
- Pass the teaching practice requirement to qualify as a teacher.

Specific Objectives of Teaching Practice

More specifically, the teaching practice exercise is intended to enable the student teacher:

- Teach his subject of specialization with the competence and zeal it desires;
- Prepare and present lesson according to a specified and approved format;
- Manage the classroom effectively through diverse questioning techniques especially a child-centered interactive and activity based learning.
- Learn from shared ideas with any professionally qualified teacher during the T.P. exercise;
- Evaluate lessons and self during and after teaching
- Acquire and demonstrate attitudes of a good teacher, which include concern for student and pupils, tolerance, warmth, and sensitivity to professional ethics;
- Lay the foundation for an attitude of continual self-development, academically and in teaching skills, human relations, relevant to the profession.
- Obtain the grade level expected in order to fulfill the graduation requirement for the student teachers programme of study.

Organization of Teaching Practice

Organization of teaching practice is one of the major components of the teacher preparatory programme. Teaching practice organization is not uniform as noted by Hassan (2010). Hassan further explained that its organization depends on the nature of the programme and the internal administrative mechanism of the institution. Which ever be the case, organization of teaching practice starts with the identification of cooperating schools and posting the students to such cooperating schools, orientation of supervisors and student teachers alike and the identification of the roles of the various stakeholders involved in the teaching practice exercise with the aim of enhancing proper assessment.

Factors to Consider in the Choice of Cooperating Schools

Different teacher training institutions have different model of selecting teaching practice centres or cooperating schools for student teachers during the teaching practice exercise. According to Vipene and Jeremiah (2012), some institutions give student teachers opportunity of selecting only the location (town) of the teaching practice exercise, while the school posts the student teacher to any school located within the specified location (town). In some other situation, the institution may specify catchment areas such as a State, Local Government Area or a District, which they can post the student teacher without giving them the opportunity to make any choice. While in most liberal and democratic setting, the student teacher is given the opportunity to choose a school of his choice within a geographical setting. Which ever be the case, when the student teacher is given the opportunity to make a choice of his teaching practice centre, the work of Hassan (2010), Vipene and Jeremiah (2012) and Adams (2013), tend to suggest some factors that need to be considered by the student teacher.

Nearness to Institution of Learning

Hassan (2010), contends that teaching practice is a period of closer interaction between student teachers themselves and supervisors. Hence, in the choice of teaching practice centres, student teachers need to consider those schools close to their institution of learning. This factor may save the student teacher the problem of accommodation and other related logistics. It will also give the student teacher opportunity to be in close contact with his supervisors and the school with regards to the use and application of instructional materials as most of such materials can be sourced locally at the college Instructional Resource Centre (IRC).

Accessibility in terms of Transport and Communication

Accessibility in this regard means easy movement and smooth flow of information. This factor enables the student teacher to exchange ideas with his fellow student teachers, co-operating teachers and supervisors alike. Accessibility is also a crucial factor that can enable the teaching practice supervisors, co-ordinator and even the external examiners reach their students for the process of evaluation or monitoring of the programme.

Availability of Subject Area

Student teachers are advised to choose only those schools that offer discipline in their subject areas. For example, it will be very ironical for a student teacher specializing in Igbo language to choose a school that does not offer the subject. If such is done, the student teacher may not have a teaching subject. Even when he wants to introduce the subject, Adams (2013) reported that he may run into the problem of time, instructional materials, textbooks and proper mentoring from co-operating teachers.

Medium of Instruction

The essence of any teaching encounter is learning. Hence the medium of instruction has a key role in the teaching learning process. The student teacher in the choice of their teaching practice centres should consider those schools they can understand and communicate effectively with the language used as medium of instruction. For example, an Ijaw student teacher in Hausa land may find it difficult to practice in a school were the Hausa language is used as a medium of instruction if he does not understand Hausa language. It may be better for such a student teacher to opt for a school that uses English language as a medium of instruction.

Availability of Facilities and Instructional Materials

The use and application of relevant instructional materials is an essential component of a good lesson presentation in Teaching Practice. Thus the student teacher in the choice of teaching practice centre need to consider the availability of essential facilities and materials in order to avoid cost. For example, a student teacher specializing in physical education should choose schools with good sporting facilities and play space. Availability of such materials will enhance effective participation of the student teacher in the teaching practice exercise. This will also enhance objective assessment on the part of the supervisors as reported by Vipene and Jeremiah (2012).

Orientation of Staff and Student Teachers for Teaching Practice

When the choice of teaching practice centre has been concluded, the next stage in the organization process is the orientation of supervisors and student teachers. Such orientation process according to Akali (2007) is aimed at identifying the roles of various stakeholders in the teaching practice exercise.

The teaching practice supervisors play a key role in the exercise. They evaluate the student teachers and as such, the nature or mode of their evaluation has a significant influence on the smooth conduct of teaching practice exercise.The proper orientation of the Supervisors on their duties and responsibilities therefore, becomes crucial.

The orientation programme is organized by the teaching practice coordinator. Resource persons are consulted to discuss issues relevant to the teaching practice exercise. Such issues may dwell on role of supervisors, assessment procedure and general organization of teaching practice. It is important to note that such issues should be discussed relative to the peculiar needs of the school.

After the orientation of supervisors, the teaching practice coordinator, supervisors and other stakeholders involved in the teaching practice exercise organizes orientation programme for the student teachers. Resource persons are also invited to discuss issues such as lesson planning and lesson presentation, uses and application of instructional materials, classroom management and student teachers code of conduct. Such orientation programmes provide a good starting point for the effective organization of teaching practice exercise.

Role of Teaching Practice Co-ordinator

Being in charge of the whole teaching practice exercise, the coordinator organizes seminars before the teaching practice in order to correct any anomalies discovered during the previous ones. Such seminars or orientation should normally cover the following:

- Expected behaviour throughout the exercise, mostly discipline, assessment instrument or criteria;
- Clarification of the roles of different categories of participants;
- Teaching strategies and methodology and;
- An overview of what it means to be a good teacher.
- More specifically, the teaching practice coordinators are expected to carry out the following functions:
- Educate supervisors and student teachers on all aspects of the teaching practice exercise;
- Ensure that adequate arrangements are made with school for teaching practices who are not already officially attached to any school and that all qualified students are engaged in teaching practice exercise;
- Source the release of student teacher and supervisors from their various departments for the teaching practice exercise;
- Ensure that dates for supervision visitation are fixed with the undertaking that they must be strictly adhered to;
- Ensure that all student supervision records and Headmasters or Principals form are completed, signed and submitted to them.

The Role of Teaching Practice Supervisors

Teaching practice supervisors are central to all teaching practice activities, and must be trained teachers in their subjects of specialization. The supervisors should ensure effective teaching and constructive post-lesson discussion with student teachers. They are also to ensure that all teaching practice activities are conducted according to stipulated guidelines and correct information is given to student teachers. Supervision should be conducted throughout the stipulated period.

The following are some of the specific roles of the supervisors:

- Supervisors are not expected to inform student teachers of their date of visit to classroom. However, such visits should be properly spaced, not aimed at finding faults but to correct where necessary.
- Supervisors are to collect student teachers addresses from the coordinator before the exercise commences so as to ease monitoring;
- All teaching practice supervisors must endorse the student lesson plan/note after editing them for all kinds of possible mistakes;
- Supervisors should take accurate record of students supervised and date of supervision, which should agree with the one in the student lesson plan;
- Similarly, erring students, mostly those who abscond from their duty post before the end of the teaching practice should have their result cancelled. The scores and grade awarded to each student should be carefully recorded;
- Teaching practice supervisors are expected to visit the student-teachers at least trice depending on the duration of the exercise;
- Student teachers should be given immediate feedback after supervision. An objective analysis of the student lesson should begin with its strength and end with suggestion for improvement. The student teacher should be given the opportunity to clarify why he/she did what happened during the lesson;
- Every student teacher should be evaluated by at least two different supervisors and final grade should take into consideration the evaluation report from the school where the teaching practice took place;
- All final assessment of student-teachers performance should bear in mind the particular circumstances under which the student teacher taught.

The Role of External Moderator

The external moderators are normally seasoned teachers/educators and are usually education lecturers from faculties/institutes of education or colleges of education who are at least senior lecturers. External moderators are expected to standardize all teaching practice scores through random sampling assessment of student-teachers grade within the state or schools, for student-teachers grade within the state or schools, for the purpose of quality assurance, comparison of standards and overall teaching practice effectiveness. In doing this, they are expected to bring their long years experience of observing and assessing student teachers of different levels of professional training to bear on standards. Their recommendation should go a long way towards improving the quality of teaching practice.

Below are some specific guidelines for external moderators:

- The external moderators are expected to come in during the last two weeks of teaching practice exercise to assess and moderate the scores awarded by the teaching practice supervisors;
- They are to act as quality control for all teaching practice evaluative measure, and ensure adequacy and comparability of the exercise to teaching practice supervisors;
- They are to attend the various orientation programmes for both supervisors and student teachers. External moderators are expected to sample and supervise an average of twenty (20) students per field centre.

The Role of Student Teacher

Some of the major activities expected of the student teacher before the actual teaching practice exercise include the following:

- The student teacher should get himself familiarized with the school records, syllabuses, scheme of work and time table of the school posted to;
- Revision of relevant textbooks on methodology, classroom management, test construction and psychology of learning;
- Familiarize with good lesson plan format and drawing up relevant lesson notes in line with the rules governing lesson plan;
- Preparing relevant instructional materials, test and other relevant teaching-learning aids;
- Observation of permanent teachers teaching in the actual classroom situation before undertaking the actual teaching practice; this is expected to help acquaint the student teacher with various areas of teaching effectiveness.

On a more specific note, student teachers are expected to:

- Use relevant appropriate and properly produced instructional materials whenever necessary. Such materials should be properly preserved, as they are considered an important additional imput towards the candidate final grade;
- Student teachers are advised to use child centre approach in teaching as much as possible;
- Student teachers whose subjects call for practical and laboratory or workshop activities must include them in their teaching;

- Except where the mother tongue is firmly in use as a medium of instruction especially in the junior primary, all teaching must be carried out in English Language;
- Student teachers who teach in shift session (morning or afternoon) should indicate this on their timetable schedule for the benefit of their supervisors;
- Student teachers should be at their duty post at all times to avoid stiff penalty.
- Genuine reasons, in terms of ill health must be supported by evidence e.g. medial report.

Summary

This chapter examines the organization of teaching practice in Colleges of Education in Nigeria. In an attempt to explain the topic properly, a systematic meaning of teaching practice with its attendance importance in the teacher preparatory programme was also discussed. Other issues examined alongside with these include, choice of teaching practice centres, orientation programme for teaching practice exercise and lastly role of various stakeholders in the organization of teaching practice. The writers believe that this singular chapter may not be exhaustive on issues concerning teaching practice. On the contrary the chapter provides a simple and clear understanding on the organization of teaching practice.

References

Adams, C. J. (2013). *Co-operating Teachers Perception on the Quality of Student Teachers from Colleges of Education* in Adamawa State. Unpublished M.Ed Thesis University of Jos.

Akali, A. D. (2007). *Providing an Enabling Environment for Teaching Practice Activities in Primary and Post Primary Schools in Benue State.* Unpublished Article Benue State Ministry of Education.

Federal Republic of Nigeria (2002). *National Teachers Institute. Handbook on Teaching Practice.* Kaduna: NTI Press.

Hassan, M. P. (2010). *Producing Quality Teachers through Teaching Practice Exercise.* Unpublished Article, College of Education, Yola.

Jeremiah, S. (2013). *Model Lesson Planning and Presentation in Teaching Practice.* A paper presented at the Teaching Practice Orientation Exercise organized by Federal College of Education (Technical), Omoku.

Joke, J. A. (2010). Evaluation Model of Teaching Practice and it consequences. *Journal of Quality Assurance in Education 1(1 – 2) 105 – 118.*

Michael, L. (2009). Towards Enhancing Quality Teaching among Student Teacher. *Education Journal 2 (1 & 2) 38 – 49.*

Vipene, J. B. & Jeremiah, S. (2012). *Basic Issues on Teaching Practice.* Owerri: Career Publishers.

8

A Stimulating School Environment: A Case for Mathematics Laboratory in the Improvement of Teaching and Learning of Mathematics

Anthony C. Nwagbara

Introduction

Environment is everything around us that affects our daily lives. Aliyu (2013) has it that an environment by its bio-geographical connotation means the surroundings' school environment, therefore, connotes everything around the school. These will include the school buildings, fields and lawns, road and a host of other infrastructures.

Nigerian educational institutions at the primary, secondary and tertiary levels are faced with environmental challenges leading to deplorable and unconducive teaching and learning situations (Diogo, 2013). Teaching basically helps in the preparation for life needs, establishment of basic relevance between knowledge and everyday life experience. Shagari, Suleman and Umar (2014) assented that education is a necessary and essential ingredient for development of any society which is central to the social-economy and technological advancement which is crucial to self sustaining and self generating processes for positive transformation of the modern society. To achieve this goal, society must cater for its educational system in such a manner that will adequately meet the needs of every segment of its population and provide adequate access to education for all its citizens, through the provision of the much needed resources, such as human, financial and material. If, according to Aliyu (2013) that the basic infrastructures in schools in Nigeria, such as classrooms, laboratories, workshops, sporting facilities, equipments, and libraries were in a state of total decay, then the achievement of lofty and idealistic perspective of the contributions of education in Nigeria to development remains a far cry.

Environment is crucial to the learning ability of a child. Because of the interaction, that takes place between the child and his or her environment. This interaction could be within outside the classroom. In tune with the principle of simultaneous mutual interaction (SMI), there is a relationship between a learner and his learning environment, that is, everything a learner can make use of to learn at a time which includes content, learning experiences and his intellectual levels. In purposeful style, the learner within the context of SMI tries to see meaning in his environment and uses this environment to an advantage. As he interprets and uses his environment for his own purposes, both are changed; the learner learns by using his environment. It is this interaction,

62

which takes place that makes the learner to perceive reality in relation to the stated and envisaged behavioral objectives that manifest learning. Interaction with environment implies doing. Nwagbara (2013) has emphasized that the learner must do something in the process of teaching. This doing consists of mental, affective and manipulative parts.

It is in consonance with the emphasizes on teaching mathematics in tune with the "doing" approach that this piece of work on a stimulating school environment a case for mathematics laboratory in the improvement of teaching and learning of mathematics is attempted.

The main objective of this exposition is to showcase the mathematics laboratory as an element of the school infrastructure in the environment that facilitates the teaching and learning of mathematics. There is direct positive relationship between good facilities possessed by schools and the performance of teachers and learners (Charles, 1994), Nwagu (1978) and Adesina (1990) have argued that the quality of facilities and environment in educational system impinge on the output and performance of the product of such an educational system. Mathematics is a dynamic subject and involves the study of order and form abstracted from the specifics of concrete realities. To be in tune with the modern trend, the program of mathematics that will survive this era requires recognition of the emergence of a changing technological environment, and therefore calls for modifications in the traditional content and adaptation of newly developed approaches to instructional strategy. Mathematics laboratory practicals is an innovation, a deliberate and pragmatic approach to making the teaching and learning of mathematics more of an environmental based and an activity laden endeavor. Mathematics laboratory practicals may involve conducting an experiment, building a model, solving a problem, making a survey, drawing a graph, or proving a theorem practically (Bassey, 2003). Teaching aids and other instructional materials at times are constructed and produced in the course of practical and workshop activities. Nwagbara (2013), has it that consequently, improvisation and development of manipulatives for teaching and learning of mathematics are most unconsciously the product of laboratory activities

The Mathematics Laboratory

Adenegan (2003) has viewed mathematics as unique room or place with relevant and up-to-date equipments known as instructional materials designated to the teaching and learning of mathematics and other mathematics related scientific or research work under the supervision of a qualified professional teacher in mathematics who readily interacts with, learns or specifies sets of instructions. Bassey (2003) refers to mathematics laboratory as a place, building or confinement where mathematical and experimental activities are carried out. In the mathematics laboratory, students learn about mathematical truths, verify formulae, and produce instructional materials and models through manipulation of tools. In effect, these activities as they are carried out in the mathematics laboratory help students to acquire concepts, principles and generalizations in mathematics. Udaku (2013) has opined that mathematics laboratory should be seen as part of school environment and infrastructure purposely set aside for students to learn and explore mathematical concepts, verify mathematical facts and theorems through a variety of stimulating and motivating activities using different materials and tools. These activities may be carried out by teacher on students to explore, to learn, to stimulate and sustain interest through constructive approach to their mathematical activities. In some situations, if the school cannot afford an elaborate mathematics laboratory, a miniature or a smaller "mathematics corner" may be created in the classroom by the teacher in which case the students source for mathematical equipment, local materials like different geometrical shapes, discarded containers or all shapes and perhaps some equipments found in orthodox laboratory.

Content of a Mathematics Laboratory

A mathematics laboratory as a laboratory is not so much as a biology, physics or chemistry laboratory. It is more than that because it embraces a workshop for the production of mathematics instructional materials. Class mathematics activities in the present pedagogical dispensation has scripted from the verbal approach to the more sophisticated audio, visual and manipulative approaches. The coordination of such activities draws strength from the use of instructional materials that appeal to all the senses of the learner. These materials form the bedrock of items found in the mathematics laboratory.

Human resources: A person with a minimum qualification of a bachelor's degree in education with specialization in mathematics is suitable to be in charge of the mathematics laboratory such a fellow has to show special skills and interest to carry out practical work in the subject and laboratory. Also, a laboratory attendant with suitable qualification and desired knowledge in the subject is an added advantage.

Facilities and materials: The necessary materials required to be kept in the mathematics laboratory include cardboard paper, clay, wood (plywood), wires, pencil, nails (various sizes), drawing paper (plain sheets), strings, thread, iron rod, stencils-letter, number symbols, beads, plaster, cello tape, paint and brush, sand paper, glue, hammer, saws, knifes, screwdrivers, drawing board, white board makers-permanent and water type, jumbo pens, office pins, gums, razor blades, surgical blade, transparent containers, measuring cylinder, weighing balance, wall clock, timers of sort, simple pendulum, metric rule, funnels, scissors, graph board, graph sheets, tripod stands, Bunsen burners, gas cylinder, beakers, stirring rods, tapes (measuring tapes), stoop watch, flask, diversity of glasses, drill vices and anvils.

Instruments that are useful for learning of mathematics include, geo board, pegboard, clinometers, conversion chart, fraction board, blackboard mathematical instruments, flannel boards, flash cards, abacus, counters, number ladder, number line stick and a host of other materials that may be produced by the learners.

Pedagogical Importance of Mathematics Laboratory

Teaching is mainly based on two major approaches namely the teacher-centered and the learner-centered. In the mathematics laboratory, lessons are learner activity based. The teacher in laboratory lessons is mainly a facilitator and a guide to the learner ensuring that good results are attained and the required objectives are achieved. Laboratory approach to the teaching of mathematics encourages the learner to discover solutions by him/herself by finding practical ways dealing with the problems and relate them to past experiences. According to Bassey (2003), in a mathematics laboratory, the teacher provides the students (learners) with the laboratory practical manuals or guide sheet to direct the activities. Thereafter, he only plays the role of a facilitator, only present to aid students who have difficulties.

The following teaching methods fit well into mathematics laboratory approach to the teaching and learning of mathematics.

Discovery approach: with this approach, the teacher allows the learner freedom to ask his own questions and to collect data needed to answer those questions. The learner interacts with his environment and discovers the envisaged mathematical facts, thereby developing confidence and capability to deal with more problems.

Guided discovery approach: in this approach, the teacher intervenes from time to time to caution, advises and directs affairs to quicken the discovery process, minimizes straying away from the required outcome. Students' discovery is self rewarding and satisfying.

Experimental Approach: In the laboratory, the learner is guided to investigate mathematical truths, ideas, facts or assumptions for ultimate confirmation or rejection. When students are fully involved the activities and challenging environment in terms of outcome and result, they are poised to learn better than when they are simply told, or presented with outcome of our experiment.

Practical Exercise: Egbeson (2011) has pointed out that students learn mathematics better by doing. The practical exercise as a method that enables learners to learn by doing. It is the best method suited for developing the ability to perform specific task that often involve manipulating and manual skills.

Laboratory work in mathematics is now receiving increasing attention. Special courses like mathematics laboratory practicals are being introduced to equip teachers and learners for such work and the mathematics laboratory has turned out to be an important place for teachers and students to interact. The underlined idea of mathematics laboratory is that students will develop new concepts and understandings particularly with activities dealing with concrete situations such as measuring, drawing, counting, weighing and constructing.

Abeng (1999) has observed that in our society today, most learners become uneasy when mathematics is mentioned. The importance of mathematics to the growth and technological advancement of a developing nation like Nigeria cannot be overstressed. Abeam (1998) has it that successive government have made tremendous efforts to encourage the learning and teaching of mathematics. In spite of this effort, he in tuned, that mathematics achievement of our secondary school students have continued to be deplorable. Abeng (1999) opined that the answer to improving the situation lies in the provision of adequate equipments and proper maintenance, good teaching methods using instructional materials and other manipulatives.

The contribution of the mathematics to teaching and learning of mathematics is indisputably overwhelming. Apart from abstract and conceptual reduction of complex mathematical ideas, the mathematics laboratory gives more scope for individual and independent participation in the process of learning mathematics. The learner is encouraged to become autonomous, work and discover solutions at his own pace. Learners are opportune to verify or discover several geometrical properties and facts using models or by paper cutting and folding techniques. Nwagbara (2013) opined that mathematics laboratory widens the experimental days and prepares the ground for later learning of new areas in mathematics and of making appropriate connections. Also, learners of mathematics are helped to practice and acquire cognitive skills needed for problem solving and computation. Mathematics is demystified and assists the learner to cultivate favorable attitudes towards mathematics. In the use of mathematics laboratory, the teacher becomes flexible in approaches to teaching by varying instructional strategies, thereby arousing the interest of the learner and motivates him. Individual differences in manner and speed are catered for in a laboratory lesson.

Instructional materials, printed materials, non-printed materials like electronic materials are vital tools in mathematics laboratory. Projected, non-projected and cline projected are components of the mathematics laboratory. The computer, televisions, video tape recorder (VTR), microscope and other ICT equipment are useful for dissemination of information and knowledge.

Conclusions

School environment is to be seen as a community warehouse which custodies the knowledge for individual, national and global development. It is a crucial port of call for the adequate interaction of the learners and his peers in the effort to gain from the teaching and learning which is the main target of the school. Agweye (2014) has stressed that an academic environment cannot be called a school until adequate infrastructure are put in place. The infrastructure may include classroom blocks, offices, laboratories which have to include information communication technology (ICT) facilities. Mathematics laboratory as part of the school environment that facilitates a stimulating educational environment has to be considered important for the success of learners in mathematics. A stimulating school environment in all ramifications offers comfort, leisure and invigorating atmosphere for adequate teaching and learning especially energy demanding subject as mathematics

References

Abeng, A. I. (1999). *The effect of gender (sex) on the mathematics achievement of senior secondary school students in Calabar municipality of Cross River State.* Unpublished N.C.E project, COE, all Akamkpa.

Abiam, P. O. (1998). Lecture note on measurement and evaluation EDU 223 College of Education Akamkpa.

Adenegan, K. E. (2003). *Relationship between educational resources and students academic performance in SSCE mathematics in Owo Local Government Area.* Unpublished B.sc (Ed) project. Adeyemi College of Education, Ondo.

Adesina, S. (1990). *Educational management.* Enugu: Fourth Dimension Publishers.

Agweye, O. A. (2014). The basic security needs in an academic environment in Nigeria. *Global Journal of Academic Research Forum 2(1).*

Aliyu A. D. (2013). Utilization of prudence interactive resource mobilization strategy in overall institutional development program in the higher education sector in Nigeria. *Global Journal of Academic Forum 1(2).*

Aliyu, K. (2013). Enhancing the teaching of environmental education for values, skills and national development. *Knowledge Review 28(2) NAFAK.*

Bassey, S. W. (2003). *Skills and techniques in mathematics laboratory (with students manual).* Umuahia: Hercon Publishers Ltd.

Charlie, E. S. (1994). *Resource utilization and students' academic performance.* Unpublished B.Ed project, University of Uyo, Akwa Ibom State.

Diogo, D. N. (2013). The effect of poor environment on teaching and learning in public primary schools in Nigeria. *Journal of Teacher Perspective (JOTEP) 7(4).*

Egbeson, A. B. (2011). *Unresolved issues in the teaching and learning of mathematics: The Anambra experience.* Unpublished B.Ed thesis faculty of education U.N.N.

Nwagbara, A. C. (2013). *Understanding guidelines of mathematics laboratory practical.* Calabar: Jutoy Educational services.

Nwagu, N. (1978). *Primary school administration.* Lagos: Macmillan Publishers Ltd.

Shagari, M. H., Suleman, I. and Umar, S. (2014). Nomadic Education as a Panacea for Peace and National Development in Nigeria. *Niger Delta Journal of Education (NIDTOE).*

Udaku, A. C. (2013). Concepts in Primary School Mathematics and Difficulties of Learning. *Umuorji Journal of Educational Issues 2(1).*

9

Environmental Factors and Effective Learning in Schools

Mark D. Otarigho

Introduction
Environment for Teaching and Learning

Healthy learning environment fosters students' academic performance. The environment of a given educational facility has a considerable effect on the daily activities of those using the facility. Students, academic and non-teaching staff cannot always verbalize what they like about the physical details of a building but they recognize the effect the building has on them. Research has shown that the conditions of a school building impact students' academic achievement and student behavior and that there are elements of facility design that are perceived to improve the learning climate.

As Austin, Dwyer and Freebody (2003) observed, the construction of a classroom relationship is a visible consequence of the construction of classroom learning. They argued that the parameters which influence the level of schooling quality achieved in the model of educational production are mainly driven by the institutional setting in the schooling system. We all know that clean, safe, comfortable, and healthy school environment is an important component of successful teaching and learning activities.

Indoor Air Quality

Poor indoor air quality is widespread, and its effects are too important to be ignored. Kennedy (2001) has identified irritated eyes, nose and throat, upper respiratory infections, nausea, dizziness, headaches and fatigue, and sleeplessness (collectively referred to as "sick building syndrome") as factors that affect negatively students' academic work. In science laboratories, especially chemistry laboratories, fresh air could be debarred by contaminants such as formaldehyde, toluene, styrene and ethanoic acid. They have highly demonstrable negative health effects. Poor indoor air quality makes teachers and students sick — and sick students and teachers cannot perform as well as healthy ones (Kennedy 2001). The American Lung Association also found that American children miss more than ten million school days each year because of asthma and air-borne bacteria exacerbated by poor indoor air quality.

In a recent study, twenty-six percent of Chicago public teachers and more than thirty percent of Washington, D.C. teachers interviewed reported health-related problems caused by the poor indoor air quality. Asthma and other respiratory problems are the main adverse health effects (Benett, 2002). Secondary schools in Nigeria are not given adequate fund to provide furniture, relevant textbooks and adequate classroom let alone being given adequate fund to purchase modern equipment to aid instruction (Aduwa-Ogiegbaen and Iyamu, 2005; Adeniyi, 2001).

Temperature and Humidity

Temperature and humidity affect students' academic performance in many ways, perhaps most significantly because their levels can promote or inhibit the presence of bacteria and mould. Schools need especially good ventilation to reduce high temperature (Kennedy, 2001). As for scientific evidence for ventilation's effect on academic achievement, two recent papers examining talk times for registered nurses in call centres found that ventilation levels had only some negative effect on productivity, Fisher (2000) found that ventilation levels in offices affected performance in logical reasoning, typing, and mathematics. The researchers also found that higher carbon (IV) oxide levels increased the incidence of headaches, which appeared "to affect student performance in schools".

The through-wall unit ventilators specified in school design, which connect directly through the wall to an outside air source and are fitted with a fan to draw outside air into the classroom (Odinko 2002) often become shelves for books and other classroom materials, which in turn restricts fresh air flow. These unit ventilators, beyond creating excessive, sustained background noise that can hinder learning, also tend to filter out less pollution than more modern ventilation systems, which can lead to higher levels of volatile organic compounds (Odinko 2002). Researchers have been studying the temperature range associated with better learning for several decades. Hattie (2003) observed that teachers seemed to hold a basic expectation that they would be able to control light levels, sun penetration, acoustic conditions, temperature, and ventilation in their classrooms so as to affect positively students' academic performance.

Classroom lighting plays a particularly critical role in student performance. Benett (2002) reported that a lighting designer and consultant, recent changes, including energy-efficient windows and skylights and a renewed recognition of the positive psychological effects of day-lighting, have heightened interest in increasing natural daylights in schools. Obviously students cannot study unless lighting is adequate, and there have been many studies reporting optimal lighting levels. Orji (2002) observed that students with the most classroom daylight progressed twenty percent faster in one year on chemistry tests and twenty-six percent faster on reading tests than those students who learn in environments that receive the least amount of natural light. Benett (2002) reports that there has been an ongoing controversy about so-called "full-spectrum" florescent lighting and some schools have been re-lamped at considerable expense to offer this perceived benefit (the lamps themselves are several times more expensive than conventional lamps and produces significantly less light).

Acoustics

The research linking acoustics to learning is consistent and convincing: good acoustics are fundamental to good academic performance. There is evidence of a cumulative effect of excessive classroom noise on child academic achievement level. These problems are more acute for children who may have hearing impediments and may affect the detection of such impediments (Nicaise, 1995). It is also generally agreed by Fisher (2000) that high noise levels cause stress. Noise levels influence verbal interaction, reading comprehension, blood pressure, and cognitive task success and may induce feelings of helplessness, inability to concentrate, and lack of extended application to learning tasks. Research indicates that high levels of background noise, much of it from heating and cooling systems, adversely affect learning environments. The Acoustical Society of America (2002) completed a new standard for acoustics in classrooms as ANSI/ASA 512.60- 2002 which sets specific criteria for maximum background noise (thirty-five decibels) and reverberation (06 to 0.7 seconds for unoccupied classrooms). These and other specifications are consistent with long-standing recommendations for good practice in acoustical design.

Building age, quality and aesthetics

Kirby (2003), synthesis of earlier studies correlated student achievement with better building quality, newer school buildings, better lighting, better thermal comfort and air quality, well — equipped laboratories and libraries. Kirby (2003) tried to identify the independent effects of school quality in a study of test scores from 139 schools in Milwaukee and found that good facilities had a major impact on learning. Garrett (2001) found that student achievement lags in adequate school buildings but suggests that there is no hard evidence to prove that student performance rises when facilities improve well beyond the norm. "Research does show that student achievement lags in shabby school buildings those with no science laboratories, inadequate ventilation, and faulty heating system". Strichrz says, "But it does not show that student performance rises when facilities go from the equipped with fancy classrooms, swimming pools, television production studios, and the like", while many studies tie buildings to those equipped with fancy classrooms, swimming pools, television — production studios, and the like". While many studies link the effects of building quality to academic achievement, other studies tie building quality to student behavior. Vandalism, leaving early, absenteeism, truancy, suspensions, expulsions, disciplinary incidents, and smoking all have been used as variables in these studies.

School Location

The relationship between school location and student academic achievement in chemistry has been widely reported. Adepoju (2001) found that students in urban schools manifest more brilliant performance than their rural counterparts. Also, Ogunneye (2002) reported a significant difference in the achievement of students in urban pen-urban areas. Carnobaro (2005), defines school effort as "The amount of time and energy that students expend in meeting the formal academic requirements established by their teacher and school" Carnobaro (2005) has also identified three different types of school effort. These are: rule oriented effort showing up to and behaving in class, procedural effort (meeting specific class demands such as completing assignments on time), and intellectual effort (critically thinking about and understanding the curriculum) it is expected that a student who puts forward significant effort in all three categories will perform the best (Carbonaro,2005). And studies have shown that school effort is an important indicator of academic performance (Ceballo et al, 2004). Effort has also been measured in a variety of ways ranging from time spent on homework with school performance (Carnobaro 2005).

Normally, schools grow larger in a place from time to time, but how this growth affects learning is still being explored. According to estimates of the Building Education Success Together, nearly 200 schools in Chicago, Cleveland, Columbus, Cincinnatei, and Washington, D.C. may be closed or consolidated because they have smaller student populations than they were originally designed for (BEST 2002). Conant (2000) stated that specific benefit associated with smaller schools in higher student achievement, an especially significant outcome given the importance now accorded to test scores.

Second, the evidence on various reforms to create small schools through mechanisms such as schools-within-schools, where large schools are subdivided into "houses" or "academics", is nowhere near as expensive or conclusive as the evidence on school size. Conant (2000) has produced perhaps to create more intimate learning places.

The soundness of these observations has withstood the test of many newer studies. In one recent and well-known study linking schools size to beneficial outcomes, Adeyela (2000) argue that small schools can:

- Improve education by creating small, intimate learning communities where students are well-known and can reduce isolation that adversely affects many students.
- Reduce discrepancies in the achievement gap that plagues poor children and encourages teachers to use their intelligence and skills.

In addition, small schools often encourage parental involvement which benefits students and the entire community. Benett (2002) identified similar beneficial outcomes. In his highly regarded study, "Smaller, Safer, Saner, Successful Schools", he argued that smaller schools, on average, can provide:

- A safer place for students.
- A more positive, challenging environment,
- Higher achievement,
- Higher graduation rates,
- Fewer discipline problems, and
- Greater satisfaction for families, students, and teachers.

Indeed, Conant (2000) concludes that: "all of these things we have confirmed with clarity and at a level of confidence are in the annals of education research". Garrett (2001) showed that small schools consistently outperformed large ones, based on evidence from 13,000 schools in Georgia, Mountana, Ohia, and Texas. Durden and Ellis (1995) summarize their studies: About half the student achievement research finds no difference between achievement levels of students in large and small schools, including small alternative schools. The other halt finds students achievement in small schools to be superior to that of large schools. None of the research finds large schools superior to small schools in their achievement effects. Consequently, we may safely say that student achievement in small schools is at least equal-and often superior-to student achievement in large schools. Small schools can improve teacher attitudes (Bakare, 1997). Small schools may be cost effective. Seyfried (2000) writes: "the perceived limitations in the program that small high schools can deliver, and their presumed high cost, regularly have been cited as justifications for our steady march towards giantism. The research convincingly stamps both of these views as misconceptions.

In their study about what motivated parents to seek vouchers available through the children's scholarship fund in the United State, a national privately funded voucher targeted at low income families, Adeyela (2000) argue that, among other reasons parents chose to participate in the program, "Parents applied for vouchers party in order to shift from the large schools in the public sector to the smaller schools generally available in the private sector" (p.16). There is widespread popular belief that smaller schools are better.

Based on the cumulative findings on school size, Ayers et al (2000) argued that making schools smaller is the "ultimate reforms" while this argument certainly would benefit from better research across all these issues and by a more precise definition of small, findings now indicate that reducing school size can produce considerable benefits across a range of outcomes-and there is little evidences showing school size will produce negative outcomes.

Figure 2.1   Expected and Observed Teaching Learning Environment in Some Selected Schools.

S/N	EXPECTED	OBSERVED
1.	A four stream school with average of 35 students per class.	A four stream school with average of 57 students per class.
2.	Three laboratories, each for physics, chemistry, and biology designed for 36 students.	One laboratory – all purpose in which 57 students work.
3.	A graduate teacher each for biology, chemistry and physics.	One graduate and one N.C.E teacher for biology and chemistry none for physics.

4.	Two N.C.E teachers to teach integrated science	One N.C.E teacher of Agricultural science to teach integrated science
5	Laboratories adequately equipped to enable students carry out practical activities.	Laboratories poorly equipped so that teacher merely demonstrates.
6.	Teaching strategy to be experimental.	Teaching strategy merely expository.
7	Five periods recommended for each science subject per week.	Three periods allotted in time table for each subject per week.

Source: Unpublished Survey Research (STAN 1986)

Class Size

Class size is an important factor in academic achievement. It determines the number of teachers needed, building design, construction, cost, maintenance, and operation, and, hence how much education will cost. The question, "Are smaller classes better than larger classes' continues to be debated among scholars, administrators and parents as well as in the research community. Robinson (1990) concluded that the effects of class size on student learning vary by learning interventions.

Of the teachers surveyed by public agenda in the United States, seventy percent said that small class is more important to student than small school size. This preference for smaller classes is being codified in law: nearly half the states have enacted legislation and are spending hundreds of millions of dollars each year to reconfigure school building to reduce the student-teacher ratio to twenty or fewer students per teacher (National Association of Elementary School Principals, U.S. 2000). However, Eitle (2005), using naturally occurring variation in class sizes in a set of 649 elementary schools in the U.S. finds that class size has no effect on student achievement. Similarly, Johnson (2000) finds no effect of class size on 1998 NAEP reading scores. Krueger and Whitmore (2000) found that students who were assigned to smaller classes were more likely to perform better than those in large classes. Adeyela (2000), found that large classes size is unconducive for serious academic work. Also, Afolabi (2002) found no significant relationship among the class size and students academic achievement. But, in the researcher's opinion, small class size favours achievement because it offers the teacher an opportunity to interact with each learner more easily. On parameters for identifying various class sizes, Battle (2002) affirms that various parameters been used in determining the concept of class-size. Battle and Michael (2002) stated that a large class-size has been taken be one that contains more than the maximum number of pupils approved by the national policy (in Nigeria, the number is thirty).

Safnol (1991) has the following as parameters for different class- size:

- A standard sized class will be one with 30 students to a teacher.
- A small class size is one containing less than 30 students to a teacher.
- A large class is one containing 40 or more students to a teacher.
- A class with 6o or more students to a teacher is considered to be very large.

A survey of schools in both rural and urban areas by Moody, (2000) showed that most classes in the secondary schools are too large. Most of these classes have between forty (40) to sixty (60) students. It is obvious that when a class is too large, tea particularly the Chemistry teacher may find it difficult to cope with the marking of students' exercises.

References

Adepoju, T. (2001). *Location factors as correlates of private and academic performance of secondary school in Oyo State.* A proposal presented at the higher students' joint staff seminar Department of Teacher Education, U. I.

Adeyela, J. (2000). *Problems of teaching science in large classes at the junior secondary school level: Implications for learning outcomes.* unpublished M. Ed Thesis, University Ibadan, Ibadan

Afolabi, F. (2002). *School factors and learner variables as correlates of senior secondary physics achievement in Ibadan.* Unpublished Ph.D thesis, University of Ibadan, Ibadan

Austin, H. Dwyer, B. & Freebody, P. (2003). *Schooling the child.* London: Rutledge Falmer

Bakere, G. C. M. (1997). *Study habits inventory.* Ibadan: Psycho-Educational Research Productions

Battle, J. & Michael L. (2002). The increasing significance of class: The relative effects of race and socioeconomic status on academic achievement. *Journal of poverty, 6 (2), 21 – 35*

Benett, S. (2002). *New dimension in research on class size and academic achievement.* Madison, Winsconsin: University of Winsconsin,

Carnobara, W. (2005). Tracking students' effort, and academic achievement. *Sociology of Education, 78 (1), 27 – 49*

Ceballo, R., Vonnie, M. & Tery, T. K. (2004). The influence of neighbourhood quality on Adolescent Educational values of school effort. *Journal of Adolescent Research, 19 (6), 716 – 739*

Chambers, E. A., James, B. S. (2004). Girls academic achievement: Varying associations of extracurricular, activities. *Gender and Education, (16 (3) 327 – 346.*

Conant, J. B. (2000). *Science and common sense.* New Haven: Yale University Press

Durden, G. O. & Ellis, L.V. (1995). The effects of attendance on students learning in learning principles of economics. *American Economic Review 85 (2) 343 – 46.*

Eitle, T. M. (2005). Do gender and race matter? Explaining the relationship between sports participation and academic achievement. *Sociological spectrum, 25 (2), 177 – 195.*

Fisher, D. L. & Waldrip, B. G. (2000). Cultural factors of science classroom learning environment: teacher – student interactions and student outcomes. *Research in science and Technology Education 17 (1), 83 – 96*

Garrett, D. M. (2001). *The impact of school building age on the academic achievement of high school pupils in the state of Georgia.* Unpublished doctoral dissertation, University of Georgia

Hattie, J. (2003). *Self – concept.* London: Erlbaum

Hurlock, E. (1972). *Child development (5th ed).* New York: Hilook Company.

Johnson, A. (2000). *Theoretical model of economics in developing states.* London: George Allen and Undwin Ltd

Kennedy, P. (2001). *A guide to Econometrics, fifth Edition.* Blackwell

Kirby, A. & McElory, B. (2003). The effect of attendance on grade for first year Economics student in University College, Cork. *The Economic and Social Review 34 (3): 311 – 326*

Nicaise, M. (1995). Treating test anxiety: A review of three approaches. *Teachers' Education and Practice. 11,65 – 81*

Odinko, M. N. (2002). Influence of home and school factors on identification during skills, among pre – primary school children curriculum development. In A. Mansary and I.O. Osokaya, Ed. *The turn of the century.* University of Ibadan.

Ogunneye, W. (2000). Continuous assessment in the school system: its methodological diagnosis – remedial implications for teaching and learning. *TNTT Vol. 1 (1) pp 49 – 54*

Orji, A. S. (2000). Falling from which standard? A discourse on the Nigerian Educational Standards. *TNTT, Vol. 4 pp 92 – 99*

Patti, N. (2000). *Exploring the relationship between high school facilities and achievement of high students in Georgia Athens, G.A.* Unpublished doctoral dissertation, University of Georgia

Safnol, M. (1991). Techniques of dealing with large classes. *Guidelines 13 (1)*

Seyfried, S. F. (2000). Academic achievement of African American preadolescent: The influence of teacher perceptions. *American Journal of Community Psychology, 26 (3) 381 – 402*

LIBRARY AND INFORMATION ISSUES

10

Availability and Utilization of ICT Facilities for Effective Service Delivery in Nigerian Libraries

Edidiong Akpan-Atata *PhD, CLN*

Introduction

This chapter attempts to assess the availability and utilization of ICT facilities for effective service delivery across libraries in Nigeria. The paper opined that since the beginning of the 21st Century, Libraries automation has come to stay and since then library services delivery have undergone changes from purely manual to modern technology- driven, the aftermath being challenges in terms of inadequacy of manpower, infrastructure and finance. The author then recommends that since ICT has come to stay, libraries in Nigeria should adopt a positive attitude towards its adoption and adaptation to enhance their service delivery. It encourages libraries to train and retrain their staff to adopt ICTs. It concludes that libraries and Librarians should not remain onlookers rather should be active participants in policy formulation and implementation as its affects ICT usage in libraries.

Library and Library Services

The term library refers to an organized collection of information resources. It is an organized and innovative unit of global media holdings. The library saving as a unit of global information resources collection must have a combination of print (book), non print (audio-visual) materials and must be linked to the internet for patrons to have access to electronic information resources available worldwide. Libraries are often established to meet the information needs of targeted user communities. Hence library rarely stand alone. There are always arms of larger organizations or bodies (Akpan-Atata, 2001). Is it important for library users to know that the classification of libraries is therefore primarily on their purposes, contents and general services they render. They are classified as follows: National, Public, Academic, Special, Private/family libraries. In all, the elements of modern libraries are: Buildings, Books, and Brains which could simply refer to as 3Bs. This brings an understanding that the concepts of library are not static but continuous indicating the level of growths and development. B1 stands for, a building where collection of books and services are carefully selected and organized to meet the information needs of target users. B2 - Books in this case is used in generic sense referring to all media of information and B3-The Brains refers to the personnel with required skills to manage the library.

Library Services and its scientific study of access to information and effective service delivery are currently undergoing drastic transformation and application of Information Communication Technologies (ICTs). For some times now, service delivery has undergone significant metamorphosis from purely traditional medullar manual service to a more dynamic technological driven system. Though this changes in the system have been phenomenal globally, in Nigeria it has only come to stay in the new millennium. Despite the late starting, as cyclonic waves, this technology driven environment has developed the library and is taking it's to unprecedented heights in information acquisition, dissemination, management and overall service delivery.

The aftermath is that the age-long expectation of the demise of books as contractual access to information in the era of information explosion and "paperless society" have dogged service delivery across all libraries types, challenged professionalism but failed so far to eclipse the vital role of libraries in what have been described in the past two decades as the information age (Lawal, 2012). Thus providing practitioners with challenges to review, adjust and update their skills, technologies, services and methods of outreach for various clienteles.

Amidst the competitive demands of the information age, Nigeria Library professionals must be used to and familiar with the wide range of databases available and use them extensively in satisfying users information needs. They are expected to be chief facilitators of the process of information storage, packaging and transfer among individuals and groups, assist in developing website for their libraries and provide detailed information of their reference sources and services on the website. As they engage in websites creation, they usually would take into consideration collections, publications, catalogues of individual libraries around the world and Nigeria in particular, (Mole 2006). Usually their role will become more prominent as educators, information managers, information providers, publishers, archivists, records managers, intelligence, information officers, editors, and dealers in information media etc. (Nkanu, Iyishu & Ogar, 2013). As trained professionals they can increased awareness among clients of available information network and assist them in the content and usage of reference information network.

The concept of ICTs

Information and Communication Technologies (ICTs) in Libraries can be understood as the application of digital equipment to all aspects of library work. It can also be defined as the type of technology that links the computer to the global computer network to make it possible for users to acquire process, compare, store and disseminate oral, printed and pictorial information. In effect, ICT embraced all the technologies that enable the handling of information and facilities in different forms of communication between man and electronic system, among divers electronic systems such as Radio, TV, Cell phones, computer networks, and satellite systems. (Ormes and Depsey, 1997).

According to Aina (2004), ICT in the library is concerned with the technology used in handling, capturing, processing, sorting, storing and disseminating information.

It can also be described as a range of technologies for gathering, storing, retrieving, processing, analyzing, and transmitting information. Aguolo and Aguolo (2002) also opined that ICT use in libraries also accomplish such receptive and tedious tasks as book ordering, loads and recalls much faster, more accurately, more efficiently, and retiringly than human.

In terms of professional services, Lawal (1991) had also provided taxonomy of library tasks from which a universally applicable ICT has emerged and can be adopted with local content. These are:

- Bibliography
- Bindery Preparation and Records
- Budget Preparation
- Cataloguing Classification and Indexing
- Date Processing
- Filling of Cards/Forms
- Formal Library Instruction
- General Administration
- Informal Library Instruction
- Information work and assistance to Readers
- Inter Library Loan Records
- Lending function (registration and Circulation work)
- Periodical Checking
- Photocopying
- Policy Determination
- Public Relations
- Repairing and Mending of Books
- Selection Acquisition and withdrawal of Documents
- Shelving and Stock maintenance

ARL (1995) further emphasized that the library is not a single entity and therefore required technology to link the resources of many. The linkage between such libraries and information services are transparent to end users. Also, Library collections are not limited to document surrogates and therefore extend to artifacts formats. With the above description by ARL (1995); it suggests that automated library can also be referred to as Electronic library or virtual library since their collection can both be accessed electronically via internet resources. Having all these resources at its disposal suggest that Nigerian library is not only exciting but also an improvement of what obtains in the past due to better utilization of resources and faster speed accessibility. In agreement with the above statement, Etim (2010) referred to libraries as the organizations that provide resources such as specialized staff, to select, structure, offer intellectual access to, interpret, distribute, preserve the integrity and ensure the persistent overtime of collections of works so that they are readily and economically available for use by a defined community or set of communities.

These suggest that modern library specifically require both the skills of librarians as well as those of computer scientists to be able to contribute their part for their libraries to achieve their goals. Without specialized skilled librarians that are adequately trained to use the digitization resources, the process may not function well. Libraries may not need to be single, completely digital system that provides instant access to all information for all sectors of society, from anywhere in the world due to the complexities involved in building automated libraries. Instead, they will most likely be collections of different resources and systems.

Integrating ICT into our Libraries

The availability and utilization of ICT facilities is essentially to fast track the processes about and to ensure that information resources spend the least period of time in library. It is also to provide the most effective and efficient retrieval option to the library clientele. However Nigeria has been struggling with a dire of technical talents to build, maintain and grow new ICTs for enhanced service delivery. In view of the rapid global transformation into a knowledge based economy, the problem of shortage of qualified human resources in the ICTs sector is a serious problem that is compounded by shortage of funds in our libraries. The unavailability of high levels of skills of labour force and finances are therefore of critical importance and require concerted efforts of all stakeholders, particularly the government, the private sector, University Governing Councils and international donor organizations if our libraries are to move with time.

Components

The use of ICT in our libraries should entail three components: Content, Delivery Mechanism and Frontend Infrastructures.

Content: The creation of high quality interactive trained staff is the key to unlocking the potentials of ICT usage in our libraries, as well-informed and consistently high quality staff that can ensure good service delivery.

Delivery Mechanism: Effective Service Delivery needs communication infrastructure in the form of broadband connectivity, fibre optic lines, table TV, Satellites link, free and open software programmes and equipments.

Front End Infrastructure: This includes computer and its accessories, Network resources and facilities.

Benefits

ICTs- driven Library can have the following benefits:

- Improved searching methods through different search engines and manipulation of information.
- Improved facilities for information sharing.
- Accessibility to information is made possible in a short time.
- Improved collaboration with other information institutions and centers. Opportunities to form consortia where they can pull their resources together and get a good bargain of scale to acquire library software
- Universal Access – people from all over the world can gain access to the same information as long as an internet connection is available.
- Capacity – there are limited storage spaces in traditional libraries while ICTs based academic libraries have the potential to store much more Information, simply because digital information requires very little physical space to contain them.
- Cost – the cost of maintaining automated academic library is much lower than that of a traditional library. A traditional library must spend large sum of money paying for staff, books, maintenance, rent and additional books, Ibinaye (2012).

Human Resources Requirements for ICT in Nigerian Libraries

Human resources for ICT development and utilization in Nigeria Libraries may be classified based on the occupational structure in the library profession and of ICT profession, or into hardware professional, software professional, managerial professional, marketing and sales personnel and support services personnel. Another classification may be into ICT development, ICT programme operators and technicians, (Maduewesi, 2013). Development of human resources to enhance effective utilization of ICT in our libraries may also be done in the following two approaches; responding to market demand, (clientele demand driven) and developing skill human resources (human driven). As observed by Maduewesi (2013), in laying down an ICT policy, the following basic factors should be taken into account:

- Human Resources in term of computer knowledge;
- The situation regarding computer hardware and computerization of the Libraries.

The questions then are: *How do we use the tools provided by the free and open ICT platforms to develop our human resources and enhance their service delivery capability? How do we prepare our libraries for the present and future ICTs usage – software, hardware and management?*

The Challenges

In a recent study of awareness and use of ICT, Ukachi (2011), provides a valuable insight when we consider the application of ICT specifically in academic library. The author provided the following data in availability and usage study.

Dr. Princewill Egwuasi

Response on Open Source Software Awareness and use by the Respondents*

Open Source Software	Aware of Existence		Knows what It is used for		Presently Being used In my library		Not aware of its existence	
	F	%	F	%	F	%	F	%
Greenstone	12	28.6	3	7.1	3	7.1	24	57.2
DSpace	2	4.8	5	11.9	2	4.8	33	78.5
Fedora	2	4.8	3	7.1	-	-	37	88.1
Eprints	1	2.4	-	-	1	2.4	40	95.2
Joomla	1	2.4	2	4.8	-	-	39	92.8
Drupal	1	2.4	2	4.8	-	-	39	92.8
Plone	2	4.8	1	2.4	-	-	39	92.8
Open	4	9.6	3	7.1	1	2.4	34	80.9
Office	-	-	2	4.8	-	-	40	95.2
KOffice	5	11.9	7	16.7	5	11.9	25	59.5
KOHA	3	7.1	1	2.4	-	-	38	90.5
Evergreen	2	4.8	2	4.8	-	-	38	90.5
ABCD	11	26.2	6	14.3	7	16.7	18	42.8
CD/ISIS	12	28.6	2	4.8	4	9.6	24	57.1
Firefox	4	9.6	-	-	-	-	38	90.5
Chrome	4	9.6	-	-	-	-	38	90.5
PHP	-	-	-	-			42	100
Perl	-	-	1	2.4	-	-	41	97.6
Python	1	2.4	-	-	-	-	41	97.6
Jabber								

The explanation for low usage is that a major hindrance to the use of the software is the unavailability of internet access in the libraries to enable downloading of the software. This is as a result of lack of ICT equipment and Infrastructures in our academic libraries, thereby denying library users the benefits inherent in ICT utilization. Same can be said of all other types of Libraries across the country. The low patronage of the benefits of ICT had also been identified by Okojie (2010). According to this author, libraries in the 21st Century have witnessed a tremendous paradigm shift from their conventional functions of Acquisition, Organizing Storing, Preservation and dissemination to creating hybrid functional libraries where Information and Communication Technologies (ICTs) and Networking technologies run side by side with the traditional model. This has transformed the manner in which services are rendered to clientele by de-emphasizing the idea of ownership while promoting access and resource sharing. However the library and Information Community especially in Nigeria is yet to fully annex and lineage the benefits provided by ICTs particularly as it relates to providing better access to information resources. Academic Libraries, therefore, that wants to move alongside this information age must embrace ICT that revolves around computers to enhance effective service delivery.

Enke (2012) found a diverse mixed of both technological e.g. lack of appropriate databases/mechanisms and sociological in terms of time, funding, and human factors as challenges facing the ICTs adoption in Nigerian Libraries.

Enabling Factors

It has been echoed earlier that library that works with the application of Information and Communication Technologies not only has the best of the information in the world, it also has the added advantage of meeting up the enormous demand for the information by users (Ekanem and Ebaye, 2009). In essence therefore, there are both external and internal factors to the library environment which will endanger shift from the traditional library services to the technological model. Omekwu (2003), identified internal factors, which serve as catalyst for the availability and easy utilization of ICT in libraries. These are:

- Management decision to introduce computer system.
- Purchase of ICT based system like CD Rom data hold
- Where the CEO of the organizational environment is computer literate or has been successfully exposed to ICT driven information management methodologies.
- Where Local Area Network has been initiated for the entire organization
- Where Library themselves champion the movement for application of ICT in their organization.
- The challenge to access and contribute to international Data base like Online Computer library catalogue; Lexis, Nixes etc
- The need to increase the speed of services like bibliography compilation.
- Decision to develop marketable information products and services.
- Management decision to modernize information services and system to conform to international standards and trends.

ICT Facilities for effective Library Service Delivery

Information as a product of research and management of the knowledge content of books, Journals; and media outputs, have presented great challenges to library practices and information professional in particular. Thus as information scientists whose work is information manipulation and whose primary tool is data, need to identify the appropriate ICT facilities relevant to their designed operation, i.e. facilities that will enhance effective services delivery. Some of these include:

- Computer system
- The Internet

- Fax Machines
- The Online Public Access Catalogue (OPAC)
- E-mail
- Scanners
- Printers
- Mobile phones with WAP wireless Application Protocol
- Reprographic Machines

Computer System: It is an electronic device which accepts, stores and processes data as desired, retrieved and prints the result in required format. It comes in types: Analogue, Digital and hybrid, and it can be Micro, Mini, Mainframe and supercomputer in sizes. It is called a system when all the accessories are attached to performed aforementioned functions.

The Internet: The internet, sometimes called the Net, is a worldwide system of computer networks. As a network, it could use one computer granted the premium or access to get information from any other computer. The acquisition, storage, processing and dissemination of information processes has been the entire business of the library profession all these years so we can be proud to say that the world has now come to apply what libraries have loved to do all these decades, but in extremely more sophisticated and efficient manner (Ekanem & Ebaye, 2009).

The Online Public Access Catalogue: As the name implies, OPAC is a computerized online catalogue of the materials held in a particular library or library system. Modern computer OPACs offer variety of search capabilities on several indexes book cover, video clips, and other interactive requests and renewal functions.

E-mail: For many internet users, electronic mail has particularly replaced postal services for short transactions in Nigeria and the world as a whole. Its resolute hardware and software allows unlimited usage with many service providers ability to read files written in HTML easily accessibility and large memory to host mails, makes email a reliable library tool.

Scanners: These are devices used to replicate or convert hard copies of information into electronic formats for the purpose of editing, storage and transfer. They are another useful tool for information delivery.

Printers: These are output devices required by computers for generation of hard copies of information. They come in different types, speed and sizes.

Mobile Phones with Wireless Application Protocol (WAP): These are electronic/ communication devices for easy information dissemination and gathering regardless of geographical locations. Service providers are many and very competitive for the libraries to choose from.

Reprographic machines: Machines in this class include Microscopy, photocopy and duplicating. They help in duplication, storing and Retrieval of usually recorded message for easy use.

Conclusions

Without an educated, ICT savvy staff, no library can reap the benefits of a knowledge based society or participate effectively in modern information service delivery. Library Staff need to be exposed from the earliest time possible to use ICT to enhance and improve their work experience. ICT need to be put in place in every library to improve productivity and effective service delivery.

The enabling factor to enhance rapid growth, availability and utilization of ICT in our libraries is the provision of class ICT infrastructure which include telecommunication and data networks facilities, national and international data bases in subject areas of the curricular. Despite the enormous potentials of these technologies to offer high quality, cost effective and timely service delivery, the opportunities presented here are distinguished by extension to which they are in used, misunderstood and underestimated in Nigeria.

Librarians and other information professionals have to stay current by absorbing new knowledge and learning the application of Information Communication technologies in their day to-day activities. Librarians should invest in new technologies and absorb recent graduates with ICT in order to sustain technology based utilization culture in library services delivery in Nigeria.

Recommendations

ICT has come to stay in every aspect of our profession. It has made impact on the profession in recent years, therefore librarians and other information scientists should develop positive attitude towards adoption and adaptation of ICT for effective service delivery in our academic libraries. Librarians in Nigeria should help formulate and implement ICT policies for effective management and service delivery in the new library technology- driven environment.

In order to acquire the benefits of ICT, libraries and librarians need to enlist the full support of library authorities in our various Institutions, the Management and Governing Councils.

Finally, training and retraining of librarians should be an ongoing process in order to enhance effective service delivery and make Librarians relevant in today's knowledge based economy.

References

Aguolu, C. C. & Aguolu, L. E. (2002). *Library and Information Management in Nigeria: Seminar Essays on themes and problems.* Maiduguri. Ed. Live form Services.

Akparobore, D. (2013). The use of ICTs in the University Library system in Nigeria: Challenges and the way forward. *African Journal of Education and Information Management* 14 (1 & 2), 123 – 130.

Aina, L. O. (2004). *Library and Information Science text for Africa.* Ibadan: Third World Information Service Ltd.

Aina, L. O. (2008). *Information and Knowledge Management in the digital Age: Concepts technologies and African Perspective.* Ibadan: Third World Information Services.

Akpan-Atata, E. A. (2001). *Introduction to Library science.* Uyo: Afahaide Publishing Company.

Akpan-Atata, E. A. (2008). *Information Dissemination Strategies and Information utilization in Oil Proceeding Communities of Akwa Ibom and Rivers States.* Unpublished Ph.D Dissertation, P.G. School, University of Uyo, Uyo.

Akpan-Atata, E. A. (2013). Information Types and Repacking Skills for Researchers and Academics in the third world. *African Journal of Educational Research and Administration 6 (1) 115 – 120.*

ARL (1995). Association of Research Libraries: Appendix II. Definition and purpose of digital library. Retrieved (20th May, 2014) *http://www.adiong/resources/pubis/mmproceedings/126.mmapper.shtm/*

Eyo, E. B. E., & Ebaye, A. S. (2009). Utilization of ICT Facilities for Effective Service Delivery in Academic Libraries in Nigeria. *Oniong: a Contemporary Journal of Inter-Disciplinary Studies* 1 (1), 213 – 224.

Etim, F. E. (2010). *The Quest for a Nigerian Information Society, Myth or reality.* 26th Inaugural Lecture of University of Uyo, Uyo. March 18.

Enke, E. T. (2012). The user's view on Biodiversity Data steaming – Investigating Facts of Acceptance and Requirement to a sustainable use of research Data. *Ecological Information* 11: 25 – 33. Doi:10.1016/j.ecoinf.2012.03.004.

Ibianye, D. E. (2012). Challenges & prospects of Digitization of Library Resources in Nigeria Universities: The Experience of Kashim Ibrahim Library.. *European Journal of Globalization and development Research*, 5 (1) 288 – 300.

Lawal, O. O. (1991). A Survey of Task Performance in Library and Information Work. Nigeria Perspective. *African Journal of Archival and Information Science 1, (1) 29 – 36.*

Lawal, O. O. (2012). *Application of Free and Open Service Software in Libraries: An Overview.* Paper delivered at National Workshop on Application of Free and Open Service Software in Libraries. University of Calabar 9th November.

Maduewesi, E. (2013). Human Resources and Technology: Education in the Days of Google, Wikipedia, Face Book and Twitter. *Academic Discourse: An International Journal 5 (1), 165 – 175.*

Nkanu, W. O., Iyishu, V. A., & Ogar, F. O. (2013). Education and training for Library and Information Science Professionals in Nigeria: Their Role, Opportunities and Challenges in the Information Age. *Knowledge Review 28 (2) 95 – 104.*

Okojie, V. (2010). Presidential Foreword in NLA 48th National Conference and Annual General Meeting, Abuja, Proceedings Viii.

Omekwu, C. O. (2003). Planning for Library and Information Centres Computerization in Developing Countries. In Madu, Ec (Ed.) *Technology for Management and Service.* Modern Libraries and Information Centre in developing Countries. Ibadan: Evi – Coleman Publishers 17 – 29.

Onmes, S. & Dempsey, L. (1997). *The Internet, Networking and Public Library.* London: Library Association Publishers.

Ukachi N. B. (2011). Awareness and utilization of Open service software in Nigeria Libraries: The way forward. NLA 49th National Open and Annual General Meeting. Awka Proceedings P 132 – 146.

11

Literature of Humanities in Library and Information Science: Panacea for Value Systems Decay in the Nigerian Universities

Umar A. Abubakar & Uduakobong Oscar *PhD*

Introduction

Humanities involves the study of languages and literatures; linguistics; rhetoric; history; philosophy; religion; ethics; the theory, criticism, and history of the arts; jurisprudence and cultural theory; as well as those aspects of social sciences that have humanistic content and employ humanistic methods (e.g., cultural anthropology). The humanities also include the study and application of the humanities to the human environment and to contemporary life, with particular attention to race, class, gender, and sexuality, as well as to diverse peoples and traditions. Humanities methods include (but are not limited to) the deep reading of texts and signs, the construction of meaning through interpretation, the exploration of material and visual culture, human practices, and the study of knowledge construction itself (National Endowment for the Humanities; 2012). Humanities (liberal arts) is concern with moral education and the purpose of human existence (Nwachukwu; 2010). According to Jewell (2011), humanities is an area of study which deals with fine arts, culture, and philosophy. They are non-scientific, have nothing to do (at least directly) with business or economics, and they are not part of physical education or sports, either. Rather they are the part of education, of knowledge, that makes for a more refined sense of knowing, thinking, and finer feeling. They are the ocean of all of humanity's deeper, more inner awareness, knowledge, and sensitivity

According to the National Foundation on the Arts and the Humanities Act (1965), the term 'humanities' includes, but is not limited to, the study of the following: language, both modern and classical; linguistics; literature; history; jurisprudence; philosophy; archaeology; comparative religion; ethics; the history, criticism and theory of the arts; those aspects of social sciences which have humanistic content and employ humanistic methods; and the study and application of the humanities to the human environment with particular attention to reflecting our diverse heritage, traditions, and history and to the relevance of the humanities to the current conditions of national life. In other words, the study of humanities literature deals with the application of humanities concepts to the human community in order to shape some contemporary human life pattern, with particular attention to race, class, gender, and sexuality, as well as to diverse peoples and traditions. Humanities methods include (but are not limited to) the deep reading of texts and signs, the construction of meaning through interpretation, the exploration of material and visual culture and human practices, and the study of knowledge construction itself. Thus, study of humanities is a discipline firmly rooted in human values and excellence that provides the spiritual and intellectual framework that makes technology itself possible *(*Aboyede, 1978; Nwachukwu, 2010). In essence, humanities as a field of study, can be viewed as a discipline which emphasizes on the analysis and exchange of ideas rather than the creative expression of the arts or the quantitative explanation of the scientific process and discoveries.

Values are postulated by Gilbert and Hoepper (1996) into the aesthetic values, economic values, intellectual values, political values, environmental values, and moral values. Thus:

- the aesthetic values are those aspects that are directly related to ideas and concepts such as beauty and symmetry;
- Economic values are concerned with the human efficiency and productivity;
- Intellectual values deals with the aspects of truth and clarity;
- Political values deal with aspects that are related to justice and freedom;
- Environmental values are those aspects which deals with ecological harmony and sustainability; While,
- Moral values are related to those aspects of ideas and concepts of administration of right actions towards other people such as respect, care, and integrity.

Whether you have been to the university or not you can attest to the fact that morality amongst the university students is declining with the increase in social vices which leads to value system decay. The decay has adverse effects on ethical norms and values in humanities that make us human.

The Place of Humanities Literature Education in Nigerian Universities

According to Nakpodia (2003), university is made up of people with different backgrounds in terms of needs, skills, talents, status, competencies, knowledge, behavioral styles, interest and perceptions. As such, Okebukola (1998) contends that the central and most evident purpose of university education has been the intellectual, aesthetic, social, vocational and moral development of able youths. Many authorities believe that the university's primary responsibility to its students is to help them attain higher levels of personal development, vocational achievement, and public service. This goal of individual development includes deeper insight into human experience through general education, as well as preparation for the learned professions through specialised study.

In other words, universities are communities of those who teach and those who learn, places where the minds of maturing students are trained and strengthened and where the future leaders in a society are prepared not only for learned professionals and tasks of responsibility in the community, but also for the living of a full life. More importantly, universities are places where reappraisal and original investigations/ new additions are continuously being made to the sum of human knowledge and understanding (Madu; 2012)

Teaching the literature of humanities in the Nigerian universities with the deep rooted concern by librarians in the discipline of librarianship serves as a mechanism for character reformation of both undergraduate and postgraduate students to become more human in their very best sense. Nevertheless, students' exposure to the activities of past heroes in faith nationalism, knowledge, academic, economic and other socio-cultural endeavours as determinants of success in life that was transcended to this generation which are unfortunately condemned by western civilization with the name of globalization would have positive effect on university students to become better human beings within and outside the academic environment.

It is obvious that literature of humanities would prepare the students to learn more about themselves and colleagues who works around them. Moreover, the students will realize their potentials, and the potentials of others, much more thoroughly to serve as agents of change, since university certification is based on character and learning. Actually, Nigeria as multi-cultural state with diverse ethnic groups and beliefs, as human beings, they are connected on the strands of humanities since it encompasses all human doings for purposeful human value which enhances quality of life of every human person on earth.

White (1997) has considered this approach as one of the great tenets indeed as the great beliefs found in the study of the humanities. He however affirmed that all human life is like a spider's web which is delicately spun at times, however far apart the spaces between each light thread, and everything important that humans do or can do is tied to everything else, therefore, all human beings live inside this web and are a part of a certain time in history, a certain place in American culture, a certain understanding of the arts and of philosophy and religion. As the human beings change as their understanding changes, they gradually throw out lines of thought to other parts of the web close to or far away from them. And the more parts of the web human beings hook themselves up to, the more they will understand what being a human means.

University and Mind Development

Developing human mind is one of the central missions of teaching literature of humanities and exposure of university students to its branches that have no concern with scientific approach to doing things in a humanistic way. Our value system should be increasingly reflected in the description of graduate qualities, attributes or capabilities within and outside the university environment. Hence, the potential for character moulding in complement with the diversified historical, philosophical, religious, music and arts among other attributes, that determines the nature and characteristics of undergraduate and postgraduate students background which forms the population of the universities is virtually a premise for concern in any aspect of skills and knowledge instilled into the students.

Morality is an activity of concern in all human endeavours particularly universities which demands for high order and skills of analysis, synthesis and evaluation, the ability to think critically, to construct meaning and reconstruct understanding in the light of new learning experiences. White (1997) contends that the disciplines of the humanities such as philosophy, history, and literary studies offer models and methods for addressing dilemmas and acknowledging ambiguity and paradox. They can help us face the tension between the concerns of individuals and those of groups and promote civil and informed discussion of conflicts, placing current issues in historical perspective. They also give voice to feeling and artistic shape to experience, balancing passion and rationality and exploring issues of morality and value. The study of literature of humanities provides avenue in which the expression of doddering interpretations and experiences can be recognized and areas of common interest explored.

It is apparent, that Omeje & Eyo (n.d) opined that for a value to be seen as positive, both the set goals and the means of attaining them should be good, worthwhile and desirable, socially acceptable and legally permissible. The reverse is negative value. Value encompasses the norms and ethics of any given society. If value has a role to play in setting goals and choosing means of realizing these goals, then in no small measure value has a role to play in the teaching-learning process. More so, the set goals and the procedures adopted to achieve the goals, in the educational process can influence the outcome of the educational process.

Albert (2010) opined that philosophically the motive of university education is to provide general education that prepares individuals for entry into the government, professions, business and the industry, or provide the individual with opportunity for postgraduate study. This has been the view of Asimiran and Sufean (2009) who state that a university is that fascinating institution with numerous faces: academic, scientific, social, cultural, economical, political, religions and commercial attached to its establishment. Hence, it is a universe of its own entity where learned people educate scholars, professionals, scientists, researchers, teachers, leaders, and preachers.

It is obvious to state that the noble vision and mission of the university in all ramifications is to generate, expand, and disseminate knowledge in all disciplines for the advancement of human civilization. Therefore, teaching literature of humanities has been an area of concern by the 21st century librarians in most Nigerian universities. But the intent concern of these librarians is the non active facilitation and emphases on the importance attached to the rooted literature and artefacts and the concealed genuine knowledge they contain. These need to be exposed in the context of university education because most rooted literature can play a prominent role in the life and prospects of university students because most literature of humanities are still relevant to the test of time and when re-explored and used from each clan, it would help in addressing the problems of value system decay bewildering the university education in Nigeria.

Librarians as Value Systems Reformist on Campuses

Librarians are pace setters in the early days of fresh students in the university system. They teach fresh students the concept of user education, introduction to use of library, information science, information literacy or any other name given to such training by the universities. To that effect, librarians have every chance to prepare the mind of young adults entering into the university and to instill in them the love for reading and the skills for using library for independent learning and research which are the basis for value system development. Omekwu & Ugwuanyi (2009) contend that a new student in an academic environment is certainly in a new terrain. As he may have used library in his secondary educational institution, but the school library (where it exists) is different from the academic library. Apparently, teaching students a course on use of library is therefore imperative, as it would enable them adjust and adapt to challenges of the library environment.

To achieve these, librarians as educators are needed to expose the students to the varieties and importance of literature of humanities study and its impact to citizenship and nation building as well on how the students will meet the community expectations pertaining to modesty in life and conducts. It is a desiring fact to state that, at the point of entry into a university for academic pursuit, students will be very much curious over certain issues related to life style. The most common is the non active policy and enforced law on dress and style dressing with the name of human rights; provided they will not violate other school rules and regulations. The reality here is that, issue related to human rights that are mostly derived from the western declaration are not doing well to the teaming university students.

Because its adverse effect is making the Nigerian students' forget their diversified core norms and values and forfeit their future to the detriment of style, clothing, language, literature, philosophy, religion, history, art, music and dance among other things on humanities that makes us human is obvious. White (1997) states that, from the pretence of Ohio Humanities Council view, humanities are the stories, the ideas, and the words that help us make sense of our lives and our world. The literature of humanities introduces us to people we have never met, places we have never visited, and ideas that may have never crossed our minds. By showing us how others have lived and thought about life, the humanities help us decide what is important in our own lives and what we can do to make them better. By connecting us with other people, they point the way to answers about what is right or wrong, or what is true to our heritage and our history. The humanities help us address the challenges we face together in our families, our communities, and as a nation.

Exposing students to literature of humanities can promote culture of reading among the students. Therefore without value concern for reading culture, Nigerian students cannot be abreast about the contribution of scholars to solving some societal problems. Librarians as professionals with vast knowledge are engaged in the training of human minds and their physical being for sustainable development and human treatment among the diverse group of people within and outside the university settings with emphases on the use of old documented values and knowledge instead of wasting much of their time on dynamism of science and science process skills.

The most desiring issue is that librarians are the vanguard of change in this modern day, to resuscitate the beauty of most cultures that are going for extinction due to so many reasons. For instance, primary source of information on morality moulding is fading due to lack of respect and poor knowledge about the value for old rooted literature in every aspect of human life. Rooted value system developed and enhanced by our fore Nigerian fathers from the rich cultural heritage are laboratory test free. Therefore, librarians believe that the discipline of humanities deals with the root irrespective of the amount of years it spends, to them, it is alive with all its attached value and impact to man.

Fellow discussants, let's think of the instances where you need to communicate to somebody close to you or somewhere. It must be either the situation created requires the expression of feelings, share joy, keep informed or warned in which one of each of these situations are carried out either with spoken language, signs or sound. Thus, the phenomena are part of what made us human with intent need to tell or display to others who we are, what we do and from which group we belong.

Apparently, Language, Art, Music and History are other forms of areas that deal with literature of humanities by librarians, to facilitate the beauty of original sources of information with a particular emphases and advocacy towards reflecting on the diverse heritage, traditions, and history to teach and engage in scholarship as an alternative for reforming young adult in the university systems.

Obviously, it is justifiable that in the Department of Library and Information Science, University of Nigeria Nsukka, librarians in the faculty and other professional colleagues in the field have already engaged in teaching the literature of humanities as a course at both undergraduate and postgraduate level of education as an attempt to bring back the glory of our most cherished cultural practices and beliefs from the worsening nature of decaying attitudes of university students and back to the rooted core value systems with emphases on the original documents that were abandoned while application in some cases altered by the crazy mentality of civilization/ globalization and the acclaimed "human rights" which permeate most Nigeria universities' campuses with the ugly trends of nudity and sag style dressing. Whether in private or public places, code of dressing tended to give a perception of one's ability to preserve specific heritage and social values in the midst of modern civilization and technology (Chukwudi and Gbakorun, 2011).

Uzobo, Olomu, and Ayinmoro (2014) confirmed that at the dawn of the 21st century, there was hardly anything like 'sagging' of pants. But from around 2009 to date, the dress pattern seems to have overtaken the youths in Nigeria especially those in the higher institutions of learning. From observation, out of every ten young people in the street, 2 to 5 sag their trousers (pants). This has led to cultural adulteration as it erodes our religious and moral values and norms which is the very essence of the African society. Though, Bua and Tsav (2014) state that indecent dressing cannot be properly defined in isolation of the societal norms or religious boundaries. What is indecent to you in say Nigeria is decent elsewhere. This brings to the fore the assertion of some schools of thought that indecent dressing is mainly due to "foreign culture." Meaning this way of dressing is alien to the Nigeria culture and is therefore an affront to our very existence and identity. It is clear that the style dressing to attract attention invariably leads undergraduates' students mostly the female gender to wear "funny" or "indecent" cloths that are seductive and revealing (Chukwudi and Gbakorun, 2011).

A cursory look into the immediate teaching and learning environment can attest significantly to the need and importance of teaching literature of humanities in library and information science profession. You can therefore agree that the way and manner the 21st century university students dress is an indication that something is wrong somewhere along the line and it is the remote causes of moral value system decay on the Nigerian campuses. If university students' are encouraged to upholder their olden value system which defines dress and dress code as a desirable means for beauty and cultural display and beliefs complemented with their devise attractive cultural attires, definitely a lot could be achieved in addressing topical issues of nudity and other rough dressing among young male and female students.

In consequence, if the phenomenon is addressed, the Nigerian youths will live like their forefathers who fought for our independence through showcasing the Nigerian rich cultural heritage and value system. Unfortunately, the contemporary university students are paying prices of this struggle through the display of immorality and non-moral attitudes in most Nigerian universities. Moral outlook of most students in Nigerian universities can attest to the fact that the tertiary institutions of learning in Nigeria have been bedevilled with obscene dressing particularly by female students. Most girls go bare, display their navels and boobs and wearing what are just ample cleavages on display, depicting size and shape of the private parts with minis that barely skim the bottom. It appears now that to be fashionable, one has to become half nude, dressed in sleeveless/see-through tops without bra (Okwu, 2006)

Benefits of Humanity Literatures to Students

- Facilitation of teaching literature of humanities across subject disciplines in the Nigerian universities will prepare students to accomplish their civic duties and responsibilities where Jurisprudence as a component in humanities allows for the examination of values and principles which inform human laws.
- The subject of literature of humanities will acquaint the students with the knowledge and ability to use imaginative and creative ideas without being over dependent on scientific discoveries.
- The acclaimed ICT and other scientific discoveries and knowledge among young adults in the university have a limited shelf life; thus, deep knowledge and understanding of literature of humanities will provide them with the tools for extending it.
- Literature of Humanities study in the university will strengthen the students' ability to communicate and work with others in a natural way. The major impact

is that Literature, Languages, and Linguistics explore how we communicate with each other, and how our ideas and thoughts on the human experience are expressed and interpreted.

• Literature of Humanities will equip the library and information science students to move and deal with knowledge sharing and moral value manifestations across different traditions and heritages more freely. Here it is a fact that critical approach rooted to history, and theoretical approaches to the Arts humanities helps fellows to reflect upon and analyze the creative process for purposeful human quality.

• It promotes interdisciplinary learning that adds value to diverse students with different beliefs, history, language, literature, philosophy, music, art, among others. Undoubtedly, Philosophy, Ethics, and Comparative Religion consider ideas about the meaning of life and the reasons for our thoughts and actions.

Conclusions

In conclusion, the literature of Humanities study provides an insightful understanding into moral, ethical, political, and ideological forces. Thus, Nigeria with multicultural affiliation and unified system of university education, its success depends largely upon ethical values, morality, patriotism, loyalty, compassion, and generosity. Humanity study evaluates and emphasizes the importance of these characteristics. The library and information science departments introduced the study of literature of humanities for scholarship in the university and for character transformations agitated and failed by most disciplines in the university settings which are not unconnected with the crazy belief of globalization and human rights. Students need to be oriented on the origin of the ugly trends of sagging which is associated with the then male America prison inmates as their symbol and a tangible expression for others to recognize them as homosexual and ready to be penetrated in their anus. Then why is it that male university students sag trousers while female students sag their trousers off- pants and see-through tops without bra on campus?

Unarguably, the unethical behavior is finding its base on the campuses of Nigeria universities and it is therefore, the responsibility of all, not only the librarians or the department of library and information science to wake up and address the rampant dressing style indecency on our campuses, curb the increasing social vices afflicting the system, restore the dignity of man and glorified the Nigerian norms and values for educational and humanistic growth and development among the teaming university students.

References

Aboyede, B. O. (1997). The provision of Raw Materials and Library Services for Humanistic Studies in Nigeria. In Nwachukwu V. N. (2010). *Literature of Humanities, F. C. Ekere (ed.), Literature of Major Subject Areas: A Book of Reading (pp 1-21),* Nsukka: Deeps Ring.

Albert, I. O. (2010). Filling functional Gaps in University Education in Nigeria. In Okojie J. et al (eds) *50 years of university education in Nigeria: Evolution, Achievements and Future Directions.* University of Ilorin and National Universities Commission. p499

Bua, F. T. and Tsav, S. A. (2014). Impact of Indecent Dressing on the Academic Performance of Students of College of Education Katsina-Ala in Benue State-Nigeria. *International Journal of Innovative Education Research 2 (1) :26-36,. Retrieved from* http://seahipub.org/wp-content/uploads/2014/05/IJIER-M-4-2014. pdf on 28/11/2014

Chukwudi, F. & Gbakorun, A. A. (2011). Indecent Dressing and Sexual Harassment among Undergraduates of Nasarawa State University, Keffi. *Journal of Sociology, Psychology and Anthropology in Practice Vol 3 (2).* Retrieved from http://www. icidr.org/doc/ICIDR%20.pdf on 28/11/2014

Gilbert, R. & Hoepper, B. (1996), "The Place of Values". In R. Gilbert (Ed.). *Studying Society and Environment: A Handbook for Teachers (pp. 59 - 79).* Melbourne: Macmillan.

Jewell, R. (2011) Experiencing the Humanities [Web Textbook] *http://www.umn.edu/ home/jewel001/humanities/book/0contents*

Madu, E. C. (2012). Influence of Information Literacy on Academic Productivity in Universities in North Central Geographical Zone of Nigeria. A PhD proposal, Department of Library and Information Science, University of Nigeria Nsukka.

Nakpodia, E. D. (2003). Managing Conflict in Nigerian Universities, *West African Journal Research and Development in Education 9(2).*

National Endowment for the Humanities Initiatives Frequently Asked Questions Page 2) Retrieved form: Frequently Asked Questions December 19, 2012 | By NEH Staff. PRINT; ... National Endowment for the Humanities 1100 Pennsylvania Ave., NW Washington, D.C. 16/01/2013

Nwachukwu, V. N. (2010). Literature of Humanities. In F. C. Ekere (ed.), *Literature of Major Subject Areas: A Book of Reading pp1-21.* Nsukka: Deeps Ring

Okebukola, P. (1998). The Mission and Vision of Universities in Nigeria: Expectations for the twenty -first century, Vision and Mission of Education in Nigeria. In Isyaku, K., Akale, M. A. G. et al, (eds) *The Challenges of 21st Century National Commission for Colleges of Education, Nigeria.* p49

Okwu, J. O. (2006). A Critique of Students' Vices and the Effect on Quality of Graduates of Nigerian Tertiary Institutions. Kamla-Raj J. Soc. Sci., 12(3): 193-198 Retrieved from *http://www.krepublishers.com/02-Journals/JSS/JSS-12-0-000-000-2006-Web/JSS-12-3-259-232-2006-Abst-Text/JSS-12-3-193-198-2006-317-Okwu-Oto-J/JSS-12-3-193-198-2006-317-Okwu-Oto-J-Text.pdf*

Omeje, J, C. & Eyo, M. E. (n.d). Value System and Standard of Education in Nigerian Third Generation Universities: Implications for Counselling .P 154-174 Retrieved:from *http://afrrevjo.net/journals/multidiscipline/Vol_2_num_2_art_11_Omeje%20%26%20Eyo.pdf* on 26/02/2013

Omekwu, C. O. & Ugwuanyi, C. F. (2009). Introduction to the use of library. In Omekwu, C. O., Okoye, M. O. & Ezeani, C. N. (Eds) *Introduction to the use of library and study skills;* A publication of Library Department of University of Nlgeria, Nsukka, 1-2. Nsukka: .Liberty Printing and publishing Co

Uzobo, E., Olomu, Y. M., & Ayinmoro, D. A. (2014). Problems: A Study of 'Sagging' Dress Pattern among Selected Male High School Students in Bayelsa State. *International Journal of Scientific Research in Education, 7(1), 33-43.* Retrieved from *http://www.ijsre.com/Vol.,%207_1_-Uzobo%20et%20al.pdf* on 28/11/2014

White, L. M. (1997). "The Humanities," *in Handbook of the Undergraduate Curriculum: A Comprehensive Guide to Purposes, Structures, Practices, and Change, Jerry G. Gaff, James L.* Ratcliff, et. al. (eds) San Francisco: Jossey-Bass, 262-279. Retrieved from *http://www.shvoong.com/humanities/philosophy/2280627-understanding-philosophy-characteristics-philosophical-thinking/#ixzz2IjyLPMVt* & http://www.units.muohio.edu/technologyandhumanities/humanitiesdefinition.

COUNSELLING ISSUES

12

School Counsellors and Utilization of Counselling Services

Agbaje A. Agbaje *PhD*

Abstract

*T*he study investigated students' perception of the school counsellor and utilization of Guidance and Counselling Services in secondary schools. The objectives were to determine the extent to which gender of the students, location of school and level of educational attainment influence students' perception of counsellor and utilization of Guidance and Counselling services in schools. Besides to find the extent to which students in higher (SS2) and lower (SS1) classes differ in their perception of the school Counsellor and utilization of Guidance and Counselling Services. Three null hypotheses were formulated to guide the study. A sample of 400 students was randomly selected to cover the nine areas of study. A researcher's instrument entitled, "Students' Perception Questionnaire (STUPEQ)" containing 20 items was used for data collection. The data obtained were statistically analysed using student t-test. The result of the hypotheses revealed that male and female students differ significantly in their perception of the counsellors and utilization of Guidance and Counselling Services; that students in urban and rural school were not the same in their perception of counsellors and utilization of counselling services, besides students in higher class (SS2) and those in lower class (SS1) differ in the perception of counsellors and utilization of guidance and counselling services. Based on the findings of the study, conclusions were drawn and recommendations were made.*

Introduction

Guidance and Counselling Service is as old as human creation. Ekeruo (2009) recalled the biblical era and cited the encounter between the serpent and Adam and Eve. To the above named author, "Creation of awareness in order to accomplish a task and take decision is what may be called Guidance and Counselling". The manifestation of it was the tasting of the forbidden apple by the duo in the Garden of Eden through the Guidance of the serpent. In the Western world, Modern Guidance and Counselling is traced to begin in the early 18th and 19th centuries following urbanization, technological and industrial expansion and its accompanying social problems which promoted Frank Parson of Boston to set up a vocational bureau in 1909 to help confused youth to overcome problems associated with the rapid development of their society.

In Africa, there was traditional counselling in African Societies whose activities involved helping people to find solution to problems which may range from sickness, seeking to know the causes of calamity, childlessness, infidelity, dishonesty, protection against enemies, herbals administration, burying or excavation of charms, administration of love, medicine, liaison with the spirit world and so on.

Among the Ga people of Ghana, traditional counsellors are called "Wutoma", the Tiv people of Northern Nigeria refer to them as "Obozi", Yorubas call them "Babalawo", the Igbos call them "Dibia", in Ibibio they are known as "Mbia Mfa", while the Annangs address them as "Awa Idiong". Whatever names they are called, their role is to provide assistance to other people in attempt to find solutions to their problems. Ekong (2005) noted that "the whole era of worship and healing in Ibibio tradition consists of the offering of sacrifices during the planting and harvesting seasons and also performed at child naming ceremony or by anyone who is in any form of difficulty.

Ordinarily, there also exists informal guidance carried out by parents, elders, family heads, influential people, teachers, pastors and other distinguished personalities in our communities which had since become a way of life in guiding the youth to properly utilize their life opportunities such as choosing a vocation, marriage, business venture, property acquisition, settling disputes, avoiding problems or going contrary to the norms and values of the communities.

The development of modern Guidance and Counselling in Nigeria in its rudimentary form could be traced to 1959 at Saint Theresa's College, Oke-Ado, Ibadan in the then Western State of Nigeria, now Oyo State. Since Nigerian Educational system is rooted from Western civilization, the Westernized Educational Service is also rooted from European Educational System. However, the 1973 draft of the National Policy on Education (NPE) incorporated Guidance and Counselling in all school system as an essential educational service. Although the implementation was not done or slowly carried out, the then Head of State, General Olusegun Obasanjo launched the policy in 1977 and established Guidance and Counselling Units in both Federal and State Ministries of Education and Units in some schools. Since then, Guidance and Counselling services ceased to be alien in Nigerian Educational System.

Suffice to say that Guidance and Counselling services are a veritable instrument in any educational system, its role is all embracing and cuts across all works of life whatever people may require help. Guidance and Counselling helps to know, understand, avoid, remediate, and overcome problems which may be encountered in personal, relational, social, vocational and educational life, this implies that it is a service open to both successful and unsuccessful people, the rich as well as the poor, the privileged and the less privileged, young and old across ethnic and religious barrier, irrespective of social affiliation or marital status and for the educated and the illiterate alike.

But in Nigerian Educational system, Guidance and Counselling service tends to grow at snail speed. There tends to be general lack of awareness of its importance. Some secondary schools which were established over 25 years ago have not yet had counsellors posted to their schools, therefore most students in our Educational Institutions within the area under study do not know what counselling service is all about and where there are counsellors their services are not properly utilized by all and sundry. In some schools counsellors are assigned subjects to teach and are members of disciplinary committee, officer in-charge of continuous assessment records with or without counselling offices allocated to them for their professional duties.

There tends to be general ignorance about the role of the School Counsellor culminating into wrong perception by students and under utilization of Counselling service available to them in schools.

Statement of the Problem

The level of decline in the standard of education in our society today calls for concern of every stakeholder to dig into the causes. Despite government and private sector huge investment in the educational sub-sector, there tends to be a downward trend. The failing standard tends to be as a result of high level of indiscipline on the part of the students or what Mukherjee (1998) and Odebunmi (1990) cited in Ibia (2002) explained as deviant behavior among students. This manifests in lateness, truancy, stealing, indecent dressing, disobedience to constituted authority, bullying of fellow student, sexual misconduct, examination malpractice, general poor academic performance and outright drop-out from school among students which culminate into various forms of social vices in the society.

There are no counselling services; where the services are available, there tends to be no optimal patronage. The researcher is therefore motivated to investigate the extent to which negative perception by students make or mar their utilization of Guidance and Counselling services in school. The puzzle is what are the factors responsible for possible or negative perception among students about the school counsellors.

It is worthy to mention that perception is a mental exercise, it is a manifestation of the inner-most feeling of an individual about a phenomena. Although perception differs from reality, the perception of students about the school counsellor is considered worthwhile for a research into the factors that influence their sense of perception vis-à-vis patronage and to ascertain to which extent the gender of the students determine the usage of this important educational service. The researcher is also interested in investigating to which extent students in higher and lower classes differ in their patronage in Guidance and Counselling services and to what extent location of school influence students perception and use of counselling service in schools.

Hypotheses

- There is no significant difference between students' perception of school counsellor and utilization of Guidance and Counselling services.

- There is no significant difference between students in Urban and Rural schools in their perception of the counsellor and their utilization of Guidance and Counselling services.
- There is no significant difference between students in higher (SS2) and lower (SS1) classes in their perception of the school counsellor and utilization of Guidance and Counselling

Review of Related Literature

Esdoka (2001) defines perception as the act of interpreting a stimulus registered in the brain by one or more sense mechanism. He further explains that the stimuli are similar from one individual to the next; one's interpretation of these stimuli may be easily different. Thus perception is therefore a mental picture of anything seen, touched, tasted, heard or felt, Esdoka notes that just as the setting, previous occurrence and nature of stimuli affect perception, so also background setting and nature of individual affect perception, which may be environmental, economic, social, educational or parental and so on. It is therefore inferred that the environmental background or school location is capable of influencing students' perception of the school counsellor and in extension the utilization of Guidance and Counselling services in school.

Zajone and Steelman (2003) remarked that individual differs in perception of a particular stimulus for various reasons including physiological factors. The perception of a particular stimulus among three different individuals with physiological problems such as blindness, deafness and dumbness are different. Benji (2006) in his submission posts that perception of person may be different due to their past experience, nature of stimuli, interest and expectation.

Students' Utilization of Guidance and Counselling Services

The establishment of Guidance and Counselling services in secondary schools is aimed at facilitating students' adjustment as it concerns educational, vocational, social, personal, relational and psychological wellbeing. Studies reveal that students who utilize Guidance and Counselling services perform better than those who are not exposed to the services and those who refuse to utilize the available service in the school. Ipaye (1993) presented the outcome of his findings on students' utilization of counselling services thus:

> *"60% of students who have knowledge of Guidance and Counselling excelled in terms of performance, subject selection and career choice while the remaining 40% fell below expectations in their performance, subject selection and career choice"*

Oladele (2009) pointed out that if our society is not to be plagued by a broad disgruntled, frustrated and unrealistic individual, students should be exposed to available opportunities and social expectations in the country through career Guidance and Counselling. Udoh (2003) studied the effects of utilization of Guidance and Counselling services in a few schools in Uyo and summed up the outcome thus: "students' performance in urban schools improves greatly against those of the rural schools". He attributed the difference to the fact that, urban school students utilize the services of Guidance and Counselling while those in the rural schools do not.

Iroegbu (2006) in his study on Efficacy of Guidance and Counselling in improving the quality of students performance also presented the following findings, "Guidance and Counselling helps to improve the quality of academic performance, students who attended Guidance and Counselling services performed better in examination than their counterparts who did not have experience of Guidance and Counselling".

Education and Guidance and Counselling

Education and Guidance and counselling are inseparable partners as far as human development is concerned. For a society to survive, education must strive and such educational programme must have Guidance and Counselling as an inbuilt mechanism in order to achieve its objectives. Elliot (2001) in consonance notes that education is that which equips the beneficiaries with skills, aptitudes and positive values that would help them to grow in the society and contribute meaningfully to the development of the society better than what they came to meet. Eddie (2001) asserted that education is a weapon for combating ignorance, poverty and disease, as a bridge between confusion and comprehension, as a dam for conserving man's store of knowledge and for generating the power to move to greater civilization, as a rocket for transporting man from the state of intellectual subservience to a state of intellectual sovereignty.

Nkang and Eneh (2002) noted that recipients of guidance services are normal persons and not individual at the extreme modes of adjustment. To them, guidance activities help the normal individual to improve himself, acquire more skills and get oriented to new situation. Counselling on the other hand does the same to a normal individual by helping him overcome obstacles, learn to understand himself better and be better equipped to handle his own affairs.

Types of Guidance-Counselling Services in Schools

Guidance and Counselling services are the formalized actions taken by the school to make guidance operational and available to students. Ekeruo (2009) enumerated such services to include appraisal service, information service, follow-up and evaluation. Anagbogu (2002) observes that referral and orientation services are parts of Guidance and Counselling while Denga (2002) identifies guidance as an umbrella term that subsumes several services aimed at facilitating the resolution of educational, vocational, personal, social and psychological problems, salient among which include counselling services, information services, placement services, follow-up and evaluation services.

Appraisal Services

Anagbogu (2002) explained appraisal service as the process of collecting, gathering, organizing, analyzing, evaluation and interpreting information or data about the characteristics of the individual in a more clinical approach with the aim of helping the individual to have clearer view about his strength and weaknesses in a way that realistic choices and decisions could be made especially when presented with different alternatives.

The cumulative records of the school serves as a veritable source of data about students, reports from parents and teachers are also useful in planning valid information about students. Other sources of information are obtained through interview and psychological tests administered by counsellors for an appraisal service.

Information Services

This is aimed at providing the youngsters or students with information on how to cope with the rapid changes and challenges of the fast developing world. Anagbogu (2002) noted thus: "A good information service helps the young people to meet the challenges of today and future. Growing up in a complex competitive world of technological advancement imposes great demands upon youth. Information service therefore helps in stimulating the student/client to appraise ideas critically to be able to derive personal meanings and implications for the present and future societies.

Placement and Follow-up Services

Placement service is meant to enhance development of students by helping them to select and utilize opportunities within the school and in the labour market. Placement involves placing them in different classes, courses and vocation, while follow-up entails re-examining how their plans work out or how effective the educational programme is serving them.

Referral Services

No man is an island or could claim monopoly of knowledge, referral service therefore implies the transfer to experts, problems which a counsellor is not capable of handling, for example if a counsellor realizes that a student's problem requires medical attention, he promptly refers him to the school clinic or an expert medical practitioner outside the school environment.

Orientation Services

This is a guidance programme designed to assist individuals to understand and adapt to their new environment in educational institutions, it helps students to be acquainted with the rules and regulations guiding the conduct of students. Johnny (2003) noted that orientation programme for a new comer in an organization sheds a guiding light on the do's and don'ts of such organization.

Education Services

A Guidance-Counsellor can ask question to test to assess the success or otherwise of a programme or treatment administered to clients or students. Evaluation could be done in two stages: Formative and Summative stages. The formative evaluation serves the purpose of identifying the strengths and weaknesses, so that alternative measure may be adopted to present the programme. On the other hand, summative evaluation is carried out at the conclusion of a programme with the aim of finding out whether the programme has worked or not, whether the set objectives are achieved or not.

Influence of Environment on Guidance and Counselling

A number of scholars have been writing on the influence of environment on Guidance and Counselling. Presenting a panoramic picture of Guidance and Counselling in nations on the world, Denga (2000) cited the works of Yusuf and Bradley (1983), Dovey (1983), Watanabe and Herr (1984) and Shapmirzadi (1990), the postulations indicate that environment impinges significant influence on the practice of Guidance and Counselling in various countries of the world, for example, report presented by Yusuf and Bradley (1983) indicates that in Socialist Ethiopia Guidance and Counselling principles of individuality and freedom of choice as applicable to American style was not tenable because of cultural barriers. Dovey (1983) in South Africa observed that political and economic environment significantly influence the practice of Guidance and Counselling. According to Denga, the practice of guidance and counselling is bi-polarized in the white and black communities. The author reports that "the government has introduced guidance services for the blacks, to be conducted by black counsellors who receive only a crash programme training and the tenets of counselling in blacks community emphasize conformity to the ruling group. School guidance services for the white, on the other hand, are provided by well-trained-experts who received at least part of their training abroad and are well versed in psychology and guidance education. The policy of South African Government is to educate the white children to play dominant role in the society and to train the black children for subordinate role in the society.

Watanabe and Herr (1998) report that Guidance and Counselling in Japan is predicted on recent trends which include suicidal tendencies among youths, high rate of drop out from school, juvenile delinquency, vandalism and apathy, other issues include workers unrest, family disintegration, substance abuse and aging.

Also writing on environmental influence on Guidance and Counselling in Iran, Shahmirzadi (1990) in Denga (2000) identifies cultural, social and language barriers as major constraints to Guidance and Counselling. He also pointed out that body language such as gestures like smiles, head nods and so on cannot work well in Iran because interpretation of body language differs from one culture to another, for example he identified that American value eye-contact in talking to each other, whereas such behaviours are considered inappropriate among Iranians.

Considering the above environmental influence on Guidance and Counselling practice in the international scene, it is inferred that domestically school location may also influence the practice of Guidance and Counselling vis-à-vis perception of the students in rural and urban school differently. This view is supported by the work of Koffi (2004) as he posits thus "Guidance and Counselling must be carried out bearing in mind the values or norms of particular society, be it at the centre or periphery developed or under developed as the desires and preference of two different groups could not be the same". This view point is in tandem with what is obtainable in our society, for example, if a young person fails to greet an elderly individual in an urban area, he/she may easily be overlooked, but in a typical village setting, such action would be viewed as a taboo. Guidance and Counselling practice therefore may significantly differ between urban and rural areas and so does student's perception of the guidance counsellor.

Influence of Higher and Lower Classes on Student Perception of Counsellor and Utilization of Guidance and Counselling Services

Group behaviours have been a subject of interest to school psychologists and sociologists. Baron and Byme (1997) are of the view that in group, the behavior, feeling or thought of individuals are influenced or determined by the behavior and/or characteristic of others. Educational psychology is concerned with the reaction of the individual learner with the class as a group and its impact on the group and the individual. Since man is a social animal, there is no doubt that the individual could significantly influence the group and vice-versa. Children in school situation mostly interact in groups in the classroom and at the play ground. Considering the definition of group by Smith (1994) which emphasizes the awareness of members of a group with each other, a social group according to the author is a "unit of plural number of separate organisms who have collective perception of their unity and who have the ability to work together and are acting in unitary manner toward their environment. In the same vein, Chauchan (2002) defines a group as a set of individuals who have shared common fate and are interdependent in the sense that an event which affects one member is likely to affect all.

Influence of Gender on Students' Perception of the Counsellor and Utilization of Guidance and Counselling Services

Gender issue in Nigeria and other third world countries has been a sensitive issue. This is due to the accusation that men have dominated everything, leaving their female counterparts stranded. The notion that what men can do women can do even better came to be an instrument of agitation for equal opportunities for both sexes in the scheme of things, arguing that women have the same if not greater capacity of doing what men can do if given equal chances. At the Beijing conference on Women in 1995 in China, the United Nations, member nations, resolved that 30% of all positions in government Ministries, Departments and other execute positions be held by women at the Federal, State and Local Government levels. Following this declaration, Etuk (2007) remarks thus: "After centuries of relative obscurity, the modern Nigerian woman has blossomed into an unprecedented kinetic force that has literally re-written the history of social intercourse in Nigeria, women are beginning to swap roles with the men folks and are even creating new models".

Therefore, this has set the state for comparative study of gender disparity in every field of endeavour. Guidance and Counselling is an educative programme designed for both sexes to help them in solving adjustment problems as it relates to educational, personal, social and relational activities. In schools, gender tends to wield a lot of influence on the rendering and obtaining of Guidance and Counselling services. Timbel (1999) quoted that where the school counsellor is male, female students tend to shy away from patronizing them. A survey of reasons to boost this assertion could be as such:

- Some presume that male counsellors may demand sexual relationship from them.
- Others perceive that the counsellor may demand for money which they are unwilling to pay or lack the financial resource to comply.
- Others perceive the counsellor as being too much academic in nature and could engage them in grammatical discussions which may be beyond their scope or which may show case their deficiencies.
- Others find it inappropriate to confide in a person of the opposite sex.

Male students on their part find it difficult to confide in the female counsellors. It was discovered from the survey that gender of students as well as of the counsellors play very significant role on students' attitudes towards the counsellor and their use of Guidance and Counselling services in schools.

Research Method
Research Design

The survey research design was adopted for this study and was structured to examine the opinions of secondary school students about the school counsellor's role and their utilization of counselling services.

Participants

The population of this study consisted of 1300 Senior Secondary school two students from all the 13 public secondary school within Uyo Zonal Education Committee. These students were used mainly because their class required vocational guidance, besides, the class contains adolescents of age 13-18 years who are in need of Guidance and Counselling services.

Sample and Sampling Technique

A total of 400 senior secondary two students were sampled, simple random sampling technique was used in the selection of the sample. However, the selection was done proportionately in each of the local government areas. The selection distribution is shown in Table 1.

Table 1: Sampling Frame
Distribution of a population of 1500 students according to local government areas within Uyo Education Committee

	LOCAL GOVERNMENT AREAS									
	Uyo	Ibesikpo Asutan	Nsit Atai	Ibiono Ibom	Nsit Ibom	Nsit Ubium	Etinan	Uruan	Itu	Total
Population size	310	130	120	120	130	140	160	150	100	1300
Proportion	23.84	10	9.23	9.23	10	10.76	7.69	11.53	7.29	100
No. of students sampled	70	50	40	40	50	40	40	40	30	400
No. of schools	4	2	1	2	2	2	1	2	2	

** N = Sample size of 400 students selected for the sample

=   sample size in each of the 9 local government areas: Uyo, Ibesikpo Asutan, Nsit Atai, Ibiono Ibom, Nsit Ibom, Nsit Ubium, Etinan, Uruan, Itu making up Uyo Zonal Education Committee.

Instrumentation

Students' Perception Questionnaire STUPEQ was used as the instrument for this study. The questionnaire consisted of two parts A and B. Part A had three items which requires information on the identity of the respondents such as school, gender, and age. Part B expected the respondents to respond to 32 questionnaire items by ticking (Ö) in the appropriate columns. The items were short and simple to avoid the problems of misunderstanding by the respondents.

Validation of Instrument

To test the validity of the questionnaire, the instrument was subjected to face and content validation by three experts in measurement and evaluation in the Faculty of Education, University of Uyo, Uyo. The experts checked, corrected and re-captioned each section according to the hypotheses. The corrections were effected and good instrument was produced for administration to the respondents.

Reliability of Instrument

The instrument was pre-tested among randomly selected 30 senior secondary two students who were not part of the sample. The reliability co-efficient was 0.89 and this was significant at 0.05.

Procedure

The researcher and his assistant administered the instrument on the four hundred respondents. Four hundred (400) questionnaires were collected after the completion of the exercise and later used for coding and data analysis.

Results
Hypothesis 1

There is no significant difference between male and female students' perception of school counsellor and utilization of Guidance and Counselling Services. To test this hypothesis, students' t-test statistical technique was used.

Table 2:

Variables	N	X	SD	df	t-crit	t-cal
Students perceptions of school counsellor	6.21		6.86			
	400			398	1.96	39.05
Utilization of guidance and counselling services		49.12	20.00			

* Significant at 0.05 level, df = 398, t-crit = 1.96

Table 2 above presents the calculated t-value of 39.05. This value was tested for significance by comparing it with the critical t-value of 1.96 at 0.05 level of significance with 398 degree of freedom. The calculated t-value of 39.05 was greater than the critical t-value of 1.96. Thus the hypothesis was rejected and the alternate was up-held implying that there is a significant difference between the students' perception of school counsellor and utilization of guidance and counselling services.

Hypothesis 2

There is no significant difference between the students in Urban and Rural schools in their perception of school counsellor and their utilization of guidance and counselling services.

To test this hypothesis, students' t-test statistical technique was used. The analysis is presented in Table 3 shown below.

Table 3: **Student t-test showing the students in urban and rural and their perception of the school counsellor and their utilization of Guidance and Counselling Services**

Variables	N	X	SD	df	t-crit	t-cal
Urban		16.21	6.86			
	400			398	1.96	62.23
Rural		56.79	16.56			

* Significant at 0.05 level, df = 398, t-crit = 1.96

From Table 3 above, it could be observed that the calculated t-value was 62.23, this was tested for significance by comparing it with the critical t-value of 1.96 at 0.05 level of significance with 398 degree of freedom. The calculated t-value of 62.23 was greater than the critical t-value of 1.96, hence the result was significant.

Hypothesis 3

There is no significant difference between students in higher (SS2) and lower (SS1) classes in their perception of the school counsellor and the utilization of guidance and counselling services.

Independent t-test was used in testing the null hypotheses and the analysis is shown in Table 4 below

Table 4: **T-test analysis of the difference between students in high (SS2) and lower (SS1) classes in their perception of the school and utilization of guidance and counselling services**

Variables	N	X	SD	df	t-crit	t-cal
Higher classes (SS2)		16.21	6.86			
	400			398	1.96	33.72
Lower Classes (SS1)		48.45	22.69			

* Significant at 0.05 level, df = 398, t-crit = 1.96

From Table 4, it could be seen that calculated t-value was 33.72. The value was tested for significance by comparing it with the critical t-value of 1.96 at 0.05 level of significance with 398 degree of freedom. The calculated t-value of 33.72 was greater than the critical t-value of 1.96, thus the null hypothesis was rejected and the alternate was upheld, this implies that there is a significant difference between students in higher (SS2) and lower (SS1) classes in their perception of school counsellor and the utilization of counselling services.

Discussion

Discussion of the four findings is done according to the following sub-headings.

Students' perception of school counsellor and the utilization of Guidance and Counselling Services

There is a significant difference between the students' perception of school counsellor and the utilization of guidance and counseling services, which led to the rejection of the null hypothesis. This finding leads to and involves school counsellor in assisting the students in their choice of subjects at the early stage of secondary school courses as well as later stage of transition from school to work. Besides, Timbel (1999) postulated that the students as well as those of the counsellors play significant role on students' attitudes towards the counsellors and the use of Guidance and Counselling Services. The school counsellor tries to develop special interest in the students for the sake of assisting them in all their problems. It is through this that the students would have full understanding of the mandatory nature of utilization of Guidance and Counselling Services. Agbaje (2009) asserted that academic success of students to a large extent depends on the counsellors' skills and intelligence in guiding the students. Markson (2005) also supported the finding of the study, according to him, counsellors' skills have a significant influence on the students' academic performance.

Influence of Environment on Students' Perception of the School Counsellor and the use of Guidance and Counselling Services

The result showed that students from Urban and Rural schools differed in their perception of the school counsellor and the use of Guidance and Counselling Services. Adetola (2001) shared this opinion when he said that students in Urban and Semi-urban areas would do better in every educational endeavours including Guidance and Counselling. The reason, according to the author, is that teachers/counsellors posted to urban schools are happier than those of the rural schools which in turn affects their duty performance significantly. In agreement with this finding, Erikson (2006) observed that secondary school students' potentials in Arts, Science and Social Sciences could only be discovered through utilization of Guidance and Counselling Services. He added that students in secondary school would put up impressive performance in all the subjects when they are well guided and when they are occupationally exposed through vocational guidance by a trained vocational counsellor.

The influence of Higher and Lower classes in students' perception of School Counsellor and Utilization of Guidance and Counselling Service in Schools

Hypothesis 3 indicated that students in higher (SS 3) and lower classes (SS1) realistically differ in their perception of the school counsellor and utilization of guidance and counselling services in schools. The finding supported the work of Markson (2005) who remarks that students in the higher and lower classes are likely to differ in their opinion as long as their sentiments, expectations, interests, desires and goals are different from the others. This goes a long way to prove that a class of students is a social group as defined by Smith (1994) as unit of plural number of organisms who have collective perception of their unity and ability to work together and acting in unitary manner towards their environment. In addition, Bruinsma (2006) conducted a research on higher and lower secondary school students and he came up with the result that students who made use of counselling services performed better in their subjects, have good vocational guidance and develop fine social personal relationships with others. Furthermore, he observed that the students who make use of counselling services with all seriousness show distinct usefulness to their parents, selves and the society they find themselves.

Conclusions

Based on the findings of this study it was concluded that gender influences students' perception of the school councellor and utilization of guidance and counselling services in schools. Besides, utilization of counselling services help the secondary school students to discover their abilities, interests and talents and these in effect lead them to better academic performance and admired occupational skills developments in their lives. Furthermore it was concluded that school counsellor and utilization of counselling services are needed to strengthen the educational system thereby assisting to solve the nation's human resource problems in the area of personality and social development. The researcher similarly concluded that counselling services provide the students with the appropriate skills and competencies that would make them not only employable but also self-employed.

Recommendations

Guidance and Counselling Services should be made available to all schools in urban and rural areas in Nigeria. When this is done, the Parents/Teachers Association (PTA) in their various deliberations should be equally made to play supervisory role by getting their children involved in various academic activities. This would give them early indication as to choice of subjects and occupational direction of their children because home is always considered as the first school.

Enticing environmental programmes should be launched and carried out to enlighten the male and female students on the roles of Guidance and Counselling. This would assist to expose the teachers and the students as well as the usefulness of vocational guidance in the career development of the youth.

Professional guidance and counselling should be employed by the government in public schools to take responsibility in counselling the students on academic achievement career and vocational choices. Appropriate counselling equipments should similarly be supplied to the schools to make the counsellor work faster and better all to the advantages of the students.

References

Agbaje, A. A. (2009). Social Perception, Motivational Preference and Employment Prospects of the Challenged Youth in Cross River State. *Published by the National Association for the Advancement of Knowledge, Benin City.*

Baron, J. C. & Byme, W. C. (1997). *Philosophy of Virtual Perception.* New York: Holt Reinhert and Winston.

Benji, T. D. (2006). *Counselling Psychology, Issues and Fundamentals.* Bombay Vakils and Sixan.

Bruinsma, S. (2006). *Fundamentals of Guidance.* India: Prentice Hall of India.

Chanchan, S. S. (2002). *Advance Educational Psychology (6th Edition).* Viskas Publishing House (PVT) Ltd.

Denga, I. (2002). *Guidance and Counselling in School and non-school settings.* Calabar: Centaur Press.

Dovey, K. (1983). Guidance and Counselling in the Republic of South Africa. *The Personnel and Guidance Journal.*

Eddie, A. (2001). *Educational Psychology in a changing world.* London: George Allen and Unwin.

Ekeruo, A. I. (2009). *Essential of Educational Psychology.* Enugu: Central Books Ltd.

Elliot (2001). *Let's Discuss Education.* Ibadan: University Press.

Erikson, C. H. (2006). *The role of the staff in the Guidance Programme.* East Leasing. Institute of Counselling, Testing and Guidance.

Esdoka, M. B. (2001). *Psychology of Human Learning.* Lagos: Brookfon and Sons Publishers.

Etuk, (2007). *Studying the child.* Lagos: Truvic Publishers Ltd.

Ipaye, T. (1993). *The Roles of the Home, the Community and the School in Guidance and Counselling.* Ife University Press.

Iroegbu, D. N. (2006). *Counselling for Career Development.* Lagos: Berra and Bann.

Koffi, S. O. (2004). *Occupational Choice and Adjustments.* New York: Macmillan Publishing Co.

Markson, B. A. (2005). *Psychology of Adolescent.* India: Prentice Hall of India.

Murkherjee, A. (1998). *Education Psychology.* India: K. P. Basu Publishing Co.

Nkang, I. E. & Eneh, G. A. (2002). *An Insight into Developmental Psychology.* Uyo: Supreme Printing Press.

Odebunmi, A. (1990). *Understanding Behaviour Problems: An introduction.* Abeokuta: Gbemi-Sodipo Press Ltd.

Oladele, J. O. (2009). *Fundamentals of Psychological Foundations of Education (3ʳᵈ Edition).* Lagos: Johns-Lads Publishers Ltd.

Shapnirzadi, A. (1990). "Counselling Ivan". *The Personnel and Guidance Journal 487-489.*

Smith, J. C. (1994). *Guidance-Counselling for the Youth.* New York: Scott & Feresmann.

Timbel, W. G. (1999). *Society, Crime and the Youth.* San Francisco: Freeman Press.

Udoh, A. O. (2003). *The causes and effects of Examination Malpractice.* Nsukka: University of Nigeria Press.

Watanabe, A. & Herr, E. L. (1998). Guidance. *Journal of Personnel and Guidance,* 33-44.

Zajone, N. N. and Steelman, B. J. (2003). *Techniques of Guidance.* New York: Harper and Row.

13

Supportive School Environment for Whole-Person Development in Nigeria: Counselling Implications

Chiaka P. Denwigwe *PhD*

Introduction

The future of any nation is pre-determined by the balanced development of the citizens, especially the children. The development of children into whole-persons otherwise known as balanced development is a direct result of the effort and devotion to duty of qualified professionals who are poised to work for positive transformation of children, the keen interest of all educational stake holders and a responsive government. These professionals see it as their responsibility to help children grow up to be whole-persons who can effectively adjust to the challenges in and around them and to be successful members of the community. This is possible through the use of a supportive environment jointly provided by key educational stake holders and the government to promote a type of education that will stir up in the learners a creative and imaginative ability, a positive self-concept, emotional stability and social skills.

Supportive school environment therefore has a central place in the effort of these professionals at whole-person development. An environment where creativity, critical thinking, collaboration and inquiry are the order of the day makes for whole-person development. It is expected that a school environment should be thoroughly academic, fun-providing, and capable of raising independent, innovative and enthusiastic children. Ideally, an environment that can promote whole-person development should cater for individual differences in the learners, and should encourage teaching and learning that are engaging. Paul-Locatelli (2002) affirmed that the education of the whole person is achieved in a learning environment that integrates rigorous inquiry, creative imagination, reflective engagement with the society and a commitment to fashioning a more humane and just world.

In this chapter, the meaning of whole-person development, school environment for whole-person development, Effects of a supportive school environment, the Nigerian school environment, improving the Nigerian school environment for whole-person development, and counselling implications will be discussed.

Meaning of Whole-person Development

Sun and Yu (2011) defined whole-person development as a student-oriented education which insists on all round development; besides allowing students to obtain professional knowledge, it makes them understand and develop their self-confidence, self-positioning attitude towards life, judgement, interpersonal skills and the like. Everard (1993) cited in www.reviewing.co.uk/development (2014) explained that whole-person development is an active learning from experience leading to systematic and purposeful development of the body, mind and spirit.

From the above definitions, it can be deduced that whole-person development has to do with raising an individual who is physically, emotionally, spiritually, socially and intellectually balanced and who can cope with daily life challenges. Whole-person development is that which promotes quality lifestyle through helping a person to develop to his fullest potentials so as to be well-adjusted in life. It is a comprehensive approach to development that targets all the dimensions of a human being. Considering the various dimensions that constitute a whole-person, such development should emphasize students' physical and mental conditions, intelligence, emotion and personality (Sun and Yu 2011).Talking about physical dimension, education should involve one acquiring physical skills that will help him live a balanced life. He must appropriately master the use of his hands, legs and all body parts in order to be physically fit. Physical fitness is part and parcel of whole-person development. Therefore the learner should appreciate the value of exercise in healthy living, cultivate overall healthy habits, learn to handle stress and understand the relationship between body and mind. The emotional dimension demands that every child should develop emotional stability. It demands a positive feeling of oneself and of life so as to cope with the stress and challenges of life. An ability to manage or regulate one's feelings is very necessary. The spiritual dimension of development leads to the development of a strong sense of personal values and ethics as one seeks meaning and purpose to his existence. The social aspect of development involves the kind of relationship a person cultivates and maintains. It enables one to relate well with others and his environment; while promoting harmony and connectedness. He must be able to cope with peer pressure positively and manage interpersonal relations. In developing the intellectual dimension, it becomes necessary that one should become creative, imaginative and rational in his thinking. The child gets to broaden his knowledge cognitively, affectively and psychomotor-wise. The creative, innovative, problem-solving, critical-thinking, inquiry and independent-thinking skills must be inculcated in learners who must be able to connect all subjects (i.e. see them as a whole in terms of their relationships and not in isolation).In summary, educating a whole-person implies the impartation into him of knowledge, skills and values that are comparable to global standard.

The School Environment for Whole-person Development

The school environment that can support whole-person development is that which allows for effective teaching and learning under the control of qualified professionals who seize every opportunity to inculcate into the learners livelong knowledge and skills. Such environment presupposes that every child can learn and so is very conducive to qualitative teaching and learning. It is very inviting, open and nurturing. Ryshike

(2013) describes it as an environment which provides safe learning spaces for students and attracts knowledgeable teachers who care about students' learning and structure their instructions to meet the needs of their learners. Such an environment, according to Ryshike (2013), tries to be nimble and adjusts as the students' needs shift, uses student-centred curriculum, develops measures to assess students' learning and employs as a leader a principal who values others, their voice and need for choice. Hernandez and Seem (2004) stated that a supportive school environment captures the atmosphere of the school and encompasses the attitudes, feelings and behaviours of students and school personnel while Manning and Bucher (2003) revealed that it incorporates the physical and emotional safety of students and teachers.

A school environment that promotes whole-person development has the culture of being child –centred in every ramification. Its educational programme is balanced to recognize the whole child and his need to develop to his full potential regardless of his personality. Such an environment, as referred to by Roberts (2007), includes the academic, social and emotional contexts of a school- the personality of the learning context, and how it is perceived by the students, staff and the community. This type of environment takes a range of factors from disciplinary policies to instructional quality, to student and teacher-morale into consideration.

Armstrong (2014) revealed the ideas of some students about a supportive school environment as one that is safe with open and airy learning spaces; has a comprehensive but student-driven curriculum, has hands-on activities related to real world of work, a good variety of accessible technology tools, and a variety of learning styles and offers emotional intellectual support to students. Miller (2008: 5) opined that:

> *cultivating the development of the whole human being is termed holistic education; where conventional schooling traditionally reflects the view of the child as a passive receiver of information and rules or at most as a computer-like processor of information, a holistic approach recognizes that to become a full person, a growing child needs to develop in addition to intellectual skills, physical, psychological, emotional, interpersonal, moral and spirited potentials. The child is not merely a future citizen or employee in training but an intricate, delicate web of vital forces and environmental influences.*

To make for whole-person development therefore, the school environment should be flexible, democratic and enable the learners to apply or transfer whatever they learn to the everyday life situation. It must be such that can produce inquisitive learners through the provision of engaging activities. In a supportive school environment, the facilities must be complete and organized with attractive and modern structures such as fully-equipped, state- of -the art laboratories, classrooms and libraries.

The relationships in such an environment must also be cordial in terms of teacher-pupil, teacher-teacher-administrator, and pupil-pupil relationships. There must also be good parent-school relationship. In other words, a supportive school environment heavily relies on caring relationships among students, teachers, administrators, parents, and members of the community for whole-person development. The place of relationships in producing a whole –person therefore cannot be overemphasized. For instance the kind of relationship a child has with his parent/guardian will greatly affect his activities in the school while what happens between the child and the teacher at the close of the school day will lead to his doing or not doing his home work properly. Students are more up and doing when they are sure that their teachers care about them, respect their views, feel they are competent and will want them to succeed. Student-student relationships are paramount in the development of the whole- child. A supportive school environment discourages harassment, bullying or violence of any kind while encouraging the establishment of social norms. Thus, healthy relationship among peers is the order of the day. Among the school academic and non-academic staff and the administration in a supportive school environment, a spirit of trust, respect, and support for one another is necessary for overall success. The existence of a cordial relationship among the staff enables them to work effectively and to impart to the students the appropriate skills, values and etiquette. School-parent community relationships are also vital. Parents and community members should work hand in hand with teachers for a supportive school environment. The parents and community should value education and support teachers while teachers and school administrators should accord them that sense of belonging. A strong Parent-Teacher Association (PTA) and a strong School-Based Management Committee (SBMC) promote supportive school environments.

In summary, the supportive school environment has clear rules which make bullying and other acts of indiscipline unacceptable to the teachers and staff who are kind and responsive to students' needs. This setting discourages absenteeism, misbehaviour, aggression and dropping out from school.

Effects of a Supportive School Environment

The school environment can greatly influence the academic performance as well as the wellbeing of the school and its members. Learning has to do with the architecture, layout and facilities of the school which can shape it. Ijeoma (2007) asserted that the learning environment can serve as a tool for influencing behaviour and as an aid to the teacher in the management of tasks; students learn better in a well-managed school environment. Elliot, Grady, Shaw and Beaulieur (2000) and Moos (2003) stated that a good school environment addresses academic learning, effective discipline policies, respect for others in the school, students' safety, and community and family involvement in the lives of students.

A positive school environment provides an optimal setting for whole-person development. It enhances motivation and increases educational aspirations. It stimulates students' interests and therefore improves attendance and retention. It strongly motivates the learners and raises their self-esteem. The establishment of a trusting climate that is comfortable, safe and supportive enhances students' learning (Peterson and Skiba, 2001).

While enhancing a rounded or balanced development, a supportive school environment inhibits disruptive or violent behaviour among learners such as carrying or using weapons, use of illegal substances, smoking of cigarettes, suicide contemplation, emotional distress and sexual immorality. It produces students who are ready to enjoy the learning process, trust and respect their teachers, are concerned for others and prefer conflict resolution to violence. It maximizes student learning opportunities, minimizes distractions and makes the overall school atmosphere more pleasant. The supportive school environment helps to satisfy the basic psychological needs of students such as safety, belonging, autonomy and competence. Schaps (2005) indicated that when there is a failure of the school to meet the above needs, the students are more likely to become less motivated, more alienated and poorer in academic performances. In other words, satisfying these needs makes the students to become engaged in school, work in line with school goals, develop social skills and understanding values, and make positive contributions to the school and community.

The Nigerian School Environment

It is necessary to consider the Nigerian situation as far as school environment is concerned. Ajayi, Ekundayo and Osalusi (2010) asserted that a number of schools in Nigeria still languish in the old architectural designs with crumbling walls and limited resources, and many of the schools tend to shoe-horn modern day learning and current resources into the nineteenth century surroundings. Obviously, in view of the dilapidating classrooms, libraries, laboratories, halls, rickety furniture and other infrastructural facilities, there is nothing to write home about the school environment. Ahmed (2003) in Ajayi et al (2010) lamented that most schools in the nation experience teaching and learning under non-conducive environment. Ajayi et al opined that the non-conducive psychological environment involving interpersonal relationships among students and between students and their teachers tend to jeopardize teaching and learning.

The vast majority of Nigerian schools need equipping and refurbishing and a boosting of teachers' morale. Aside from the infrastructural facilities being in very poor conditions, they cannot support the increasing student enrolment. Amenities meant for a fewer number of learners have to be shared by many as there is a resultant overcrowding. Amenities like electricity and potable water are not always there. Most often due to lack of electricity and water, schools fail to install and use their equipment for vocational workshops where available. There is also a dearth in the availability of trained personnel to run and maintain the equipment. Most schools that have computers and other laboratory equipment have them locked up without putting them to use and with time they develop faults due to disuse.Lack of infrastructural facilities in the schools results to overcrowding and therefore causes poor teaching and learning. Unwholesome practices such as admission racketing especially in the higher institutions, and examination malpractices also result. As pointed out by Saheed (2013), the implications of the school environments being dotted with dilapidated buildings equipped with outdated laboratory facilities without adequate ventilation may be crippling and result in low morale and poor teaching performance. This in turn may translate to students' poor performance in examination, examination malpractice, cultism and other vices detrimental to social cohesion and peaceful coexistence in the society. However, teachers like well-structured and ventilated classroom designs. Donald (2009) opined that a classroom furnished and flourished with equipment that can cause, channel, sustain and influence teachers' behaviour towards high performance in schools should be planned for.Another problem is that the issues of accountability and standardization are held uppermost by policy makers, parents and school officials such that teachers are told what to do to measure up without allowing them opportunity for creativity, adjustment and adaptation. Providing the schools and teachers with the space and resources to innovate and adjust to the prevailing circumstances so as to be able to meet with the needs of their students is very important.

Improving the Nigerian School Environment for Whole-person Development

To improve the Nigerian school environment for whole-person development, a lot needs to be done. First and foremost, the infrastructural facilities must be in place and maintained regularly. The curriculum should be such that lessons and learning experiences focus on various aspects of the students while rote-learning through note-taking and lecture should be down-played. Meaningful learning should be promoted over and above learning to pass examinations. This means that learning that can be transferred or applied in everyday life situations should be encouraged. Learning therefore should emphasize self-evaluation rather than grading.

The teacher should play the role of a facilitator by being supportive, understanding and genuine. He should not be critical, hostile and judgemental. He is expected to create an engaging environment where inquiry-based questions that encourage meaningful learning are put forward. He should be mindful of individual differences among the learners and therefore carry all learners along by ensuring that his lessons positively impact on the three categories of learners namely the visual, auditory and kinaesthetic learners. For the teacher to effectively do these, he needs adequate training and retraining. Government therefore should ensure that the teacher training curriculum is enriched while regular training workshops are planned for the in-service teachers. All educational experiences should be tailored to the developmental level of the learners rather than the individual being tailored to suit the environment. Therefore varieties of extracurricular activities, opportunities for excursions, and communication-based projects should be provided.Active learning strategies such as cooperative learning and project-based learning should be adopted. It is always good to employ differentiated instruction which according to Tomlinson (2005) is a philosophy of teaching based on the premise that students learn best when their teachers accommodate the differences in their readiness levels, interests and learning profiles. Tomlinson (2005) further stated that content, process and product are the three elements guiding differentiated instructions. Content here connotes that the students are given access to the same subject matter but allowed to master it in different ways while process refers to the ways in which the content is taught. Product refers to how the students demonstrate their understanding. Aside from improving the infrastructural facilities, improving teaching and learning and training and retraining of teachers, there should also be increased community involvement, award of scholarships, establishment of ICT/creativity centres, support for early childcare developments and infrastructural improvements. The issue of universality, equity, quality education and infrastructural development must be emphasized.

Counselling Implications

The issue of providing a supportive school environment for whole-person development implies that school counsellors have a crucial role to play. Bitzman (2005) believed that school counsellors hold a leadership role in the development, implementation and maintenance of school environment. School counsellors therefore are expected to promote a supportive school environment by:

- Utilizing their knowledge of counselling, classroom guidance, consultation and advocacy.
- Applying their qualities of flexibility, affective health, open-mindedness, self-directedness, and empathy, ability to care, adapt and collaborate.
- Employing their training skills in communication, relationship building, referral assistance and reinforcement techniques.
- Coordinating the relevant school guidance services.
- Collaborating with all stakeholders such as administrators, school personnel, parents/caregivers, students and community members, etc.

Conclusion

Education for the development of the whole-person presupposes that the child as an active and not a passive learner deserves to learn under a supportive environment that will bring out his hidden potentials and make him useful in his society. In ensuring a supportive environment the place of cordial relationships among parents, teacing and non-teaching staff, school administrators, government and the community is very important. Adequate facilities are also very key to the development of a supportive school environment.

References

Ahmed, T. M. (2003). Education and National Development in Nigeria. *Journal of Studies in Education, 10:35-36.*

Ajayi, I. A., Ekundayo, H. T., & Osalusi, F. M. (2010). Learning Environment and Secondary School Effectiveness in Nigeria. *Www. Knepublishers.com/.../HCS-4-3-137-Ajayi-1-A-Tt.pdf.* Retrieved on 4th October, 2014.

Armstrong, S. (2014). What makes a Good School: Students speak up at a Leadership Forum. Retrieved from www.edutopia.org/what- makes-good-school, on 4ty October, 2014.

Bitzman, M. (2005). Improving Our Moral Landscape via Character Education: An Opportunity for School Counsellor Leadership. *Professional School Counselling, 8, 293-296.*

Elliot, D., Grady, J., Shaw, T. & Beaulieur, M. (2000). *Safe Communities, Safe School Planning Guide: A Tool for Community Violence Prevention.* Boulder, CO: Institute of Behavioural Science, University of Colorado.

Everard, K. B. (1993). The History of Development Training. Publisher: Chair of Development training Advisory Group. In Greenway, R. (2010). Reviewing Skills Training. *reviewing.co.uk-/development. training/definitions.htm.* Retrieved 13th October, 2014.

Hernandez, T. J. & Seem, S. R. (2004). A Safe School Climate: A Systematic Approach and the School Counsellor. *Professional School Counselling, 7, 256-263.*

Ijeoma, M. E. (2007). Students' Perception of their Classroom. *Lagos Journal of Educational Administration and Planning, 3(1): 145-152.*

Manning, M. L., & Bucher, K. T. (2003). *Classroom Management models, Applications and Cases.* Upper Saddle River, N.J: Prentice Hall.

Miller, R. (2008). *The Self-organizing Revolution: Common Principles of the Educational Alternatives' Movement*s. Brandon, VT Holistic Education Press.

Moos, R. (2003). Social Contexts: Transcending their Power and their Fragility. *American Journal of Community Psychology, 31, 1-13.*

Paul-Locatelli, S. J. (2002). Santa Clara's Tapestry of Excellence: The Education of the Whole-person. *www.scu.edu./president/reports/2002/edu.* Retrieved on 13th of October, 2014.

Peterson, R., & Skiba, R. (2001). Creating School Climates that Prevent School Violence. *Preventing school Failure, 44, 122-130.*

Roberts, B. (2007). Best Practices: Building Blocks for Enhancing School Environment. John Hopkins Bloovaberg School of Public Health, Baltimore, Maryland.*Www. jhsph.edu/research/centers-and.../best-practicals-monograph.pdf. Retrieved 4ᵗʰ October, 2014.*

Ryshike, R. (2013). What Qualities make for an Ideal School or Classroom? *Irryshike. wordpress.com/-/what-qualities-make-for-an-ideal-school-or-classroom.* Retrieved 4ᵗʰ October, 2014.

Saheed, O. O. (2013). Classroom Design and Teachers' Performance in Selected Secondary Schools in Ogun State, Nigeria. *Redeemers' University Journal of Management and Social Sciences, 1 (2).*

Schaps, E. (2005). The Role of Supportive School Environment in promoting Academic Success. *www.devstu.org/research-articles-an....* Retrieved 13ᵗʰ October, 2014.

Sun, M., & Yu, T. (2011). Education for Raising a Whole-Person. In: World year book of Education. Yates, L. & Gaumet, M. (Editors). *books.google.co.za/ books?isbn=1136822720. Retrieved13ᵗʰ October, 2014.*

Teacher net, (2008). Creating a Learning Environment for the Twenty First Century. *http//www.teachernet.gov.uk/teaching and learning/library/learningenvironment.* Retrieved on the 4ᵗʰ of October, 2014.

Tomlinson, C. A. (2005). Grading and Differentiation: Paradox or Good practice. *Theory into Practice, 44(3), 262-269.*

QUALITY ASSURANCE ISSUES

14

Quality Assurance Mechanisms towards Organizational Transformation: Best Practices of an Autonomous University in the Philippines

Esmenia R. Javier, *MMT, MBA, PhD*

Introduction

Producing quality products and services usually happens in organizations that work hard towards organizational transformation. Organizational transformation takes place when there is a change in the way the business is done or when there is a re-engineering or restructuring of programs and activities. Along with the structural changes, the attitude of the employees, their perspectives as well as the culture of the organization undergoes a significant change. It's about re-modelling an organization in its entirety (organizational transformation).

Lyceum of the Philippines University- Batangas (LPU-B), an autonomous educational institution in the Southern Tagalog region of the Philippines is aimed at giving quality education since its foundation in 1966. The approach that LPU-B embraced to ensure that there are quality programs and services being offered to its customers, comprising of students and their parents is the implementation of several quality assurance tools. Quality assurance (QA) is a process-centered approach to ensuring that a company or organization is providing the best possible products or services. It is related to quality control, which focuses on the end result, or an evaluation of the processes that lead to good results. Among the parts of the process that are considered in QA are planning, design, development, production and service (Ravhudzulo, 2012). Quality assurance is about ensuring that there are mechanisms, procedures and processes in place to ensure that the desired quality, however defined and measured, is delivered (CMO # 46, 2012). Compared with quality control, it has a wider concept that covers policies, and systematic activities implemented within a quality system. QA frameworks include, but are not limited to: determination of adequate technical requirement of inputs and outputs; certification and rating of suppliers; audit of the process quality; evaluation of the process established, required corrective response; audit of the final output for conformance for technical, reliability, maintainability, and performance requirements *(quality assurance)*. The study conducted by Smith (2011) on quality assurance practices confirms that there are benefits, costs and significant potential risks for maintaining reliable corporate data, and many organizations do not display the appropriate attitude about ensuring high-quality data. This study pointed out that the success in business of quality assurance practitioners hinges on quality product accuracy, data management, and service readiness. The study further advocates that the support for quality efforts comes from the top management of the business organization, through investment in the capital and people necessary to run the business. Results expected for the practice of quality assurance tools are organizational excellence that thrive in their respective niches (Smith, 2011).

LPU-B has been embracing various quality assurance tools since 1997. LPU-B, formerly Lyceum of Batangas, aims to be a recognized university in the Asia Pacific Region by 2022. With the capsulized mission of "excellence in all things, for God and country (Pro Deo Et Patria), LPU-B has pursued excellence and quality education, through four major quality assurance mechanisms such as: *local accreditation of majority of its program offerings under the Philippine Association of Colleges and Universities-Commission on Accreditation (PACU-COA);implementation of the international standards of Quality Management System (QMS:ISO 9000:2008);implementation of Investors in People (IiP) standard, an international quality assurance tool focused on best practices in people management,* and the *practice of the Philippine Quality Award (PQA) principles, which is patterned after the international framework of Malcolm Baldrige.*

These quality assurance frameworks compelled the top management of LPU-B to draft an integrated framework for organizational excellence that served as guide of the University for the design of the five-year Strategic Plan. The Strategic Plan in turn is the basis for the creation of measurable milestones towards realization of vision that is: *To be a recognized University in the Asia Pacific Region by 2022.*

This study is intended to briefly describe the standards of the four quality assurance frameworks that LPU-B implements. It will also describe the best practices of LPU-B through the operationalization of these quality assurance frameworks. It likewise aims to highlight the organizational transformation that LPU-B experiences out of these quality assurance practices.

Program Accreditation

Accreditation is the voluntary formal recognition of an educational program or institution as possessing high level of quality or excellence based on the analysis of the merits of its educational operations in attaining its objectives and its role in the community that it serves. It is both a process and a result. The process involves peer - review of the established set of criteria and procedures by a group of fellow educators who are trained to assess the criteria, and for which the program or institutions will be judged. The result is a certification by which the quality of the program of an educational institution is affirmed. The school is surveyed and evaluated in terms of the appropriateness of its philosophy and objectives assessed and the degree and competence with which it achieves it goals. (PACUCOA Accreditation Manual, 2012).

To date, LPU-B has been granted the ***institutional accreditation award*** by its accrediting body, the PACUCOA. This means that the University is able to successfully pass the meticulous eligibility criteria to obtain the award, which include the following:

the Arts and Sciences, Business and Education programs should have been granted Level III reaccredited status; for stand alone or monolithic institutions which do not offer the traditional courses such as Arts and Sciences, Business and Education, its core program/s must be on Level III status. Included in the criteria is that at least one of the programs should have been granted level IV accredited status. Very important criterion is that 75% of the HEI's program offerings should be accredited with at least Level I or Level II status. Program offerings where there are no existing PACUCOA evaluation instruments, as well as the new program offerings which do not have three batches of graduates yet will not be included in the computation of 75%. Additionally, majority of the total student population should be enrolled in the accredited programs. Also included as a criterion for the institutional accreditation award is that the performance of graduates in licensure examinations in the accredited programs should be at par with or above the national passing average for at least five consecutive board examinations. PACUCOA also requires that educational institution should have well developed quality assurance mechanisms (PACUCOA Manual, 2012).

LPU-B obtained an impressive score card in the voluntary accreditation process where 80% of its programs obtained accredited status, and two programs, BS Accountancy and BS Administration, obtained Level 4 status. These accomplishments exceed the eligibility criteria set by the PACUCOA.

Quality Management System- ISO 9001:2008

QMS ISO 9001:2008 is an internationally recognized standard with focus on quality management of an institution's processes (process approach). LPU-B,s QMS has been certified to be compliant with the standards of ISO 9001:2008 by the international certifying body DetNorkesVeritas (DNV) since 2006. For its six years of implementation, LPU-B has consistently shown full compliance with the ISO 9001 standards with zero non-conformance thus, successfully passing the surveillance external audit every year. The principles of total quality management such as: *continuous improvements for customer satisfaction* serve as the daily guiding norms of the employees in the discharge of their respective functions. Quality circles are established whose main function is to identify continuous improvement activities that will support higher level of customer satisfaction. There is a periodic evaluation of services being rendered by the work units with students as the respondents, aptly called Customer Satisfaction Measurement (CSM). The result of the CSM for the last five years (2010-2014) is Highly Satisfied (WM=4.48). Additionally, there are programs and activities designed to strengthen the customer relationship management, such as the creation of customer feedbacks mechanisms through the VIEWS (Very Important Expressions of Wise Suggestions), where students are free to voice out their suggestion through the VIEWS boxes located in conspicuous places inside the University. There is also the customer complaint process where students can officially log their complaints in the institutional forms managed by the Quality Assurance office. Students are also given the opportunity to evaluate the performance of their faculty members. There are exit interviews of the graduating students who evaluate their curriculum, services rendered by the Dean, and other work units who served them during their stay in the school. There are other forms of programs and services that strengthen the customer relations and customer engagement such as the President's Hour where student leaders are given the chance to have a meeting with the President of the University. Through these approaches, the employees who are process owners in their respective work units have become aware that customers or the students are the best judges of the services they render. Everyone in LPU-B recognizes that the customers are the most important personalities in the campus, and therefore, their needs and satisfaction have to be met at all times.

The principles of Plan, Do, Check, Act (PDCA) common to all quality assurance mechanisms in LPU-B are also being faithfully implemented by all work units. There are four important wildly important goals (WIGS) set by the management being monitored and measured on a periodic basis. The WIGS are aligned with the trifold functions of Instruction, Research and Community Extension, and patterned with the balanced score card serve as a guide of all the Deans and Department Heads in the crafting of their operational plans. There is a semestral Measurement, Analysis, and Improvement (MAI) which is later called the Mid-Semestral Performance Review (MSPR) report submitted by all work units to determine the gaps between the plans and the actual performance. The MSPR is being presented to the President in terms of the WIGS, by the assigned Deans and Department Heads. With the measurable goals and targets that are periodically reviewed, employees know exactly what are the gaps between targets and goals and the actual performance. This practice is a sure way to track LPU-B institutional performance. The MSPR periodic presentations serve not only as a way of giving inputs to the planning participants, it is also a good venue for bonding and fellowship of Deans and Department Heads.

Investors in People Certification

Meanwhile, the Investors in People (IiP) standard is an internationally recognized business improvement tool designed to advance the organization's performance through its employees. It helps organizations to improve performance and realize objectives through the management and development of people (Investors in People, 2012). These ten best practices under IiP are business planning strategy; learning and development strategy; people management strategy; leadership management strategy; management effectiveness; recognition and rewards; involvement and empowerment; learning and development; performance measurement, and continuous improvement. LPU- B is considered as the first University in the country with Investors in People recognition. The IiP framework serves as guide of LPU-B in the overall management of its human resource.

An enlightened empowerment is necessary to be able to implement various quality assurance mechanisms in an institution. In LPU-B, people are empowered through various approaches, and notable of which is the capability building of the employees through the learning and development (LED) programs. LED is about attending to seminars outside and inside the University; leadership and membership in various professional organizations; continuous education program (those who need to pursue their master's and doctoral degrees), and others. The LED activities and programs are always aligned to the trifold functions of the University, such as Instruction, Research, and Community extension programs. Within the realm of the core values of the University, such as: *God-centeredness, Leadership, Integrity, and Nationalism (LIN)*,the employees, with the able support of the top management, are able to grasp the full implementation of the various quality assurance mechanisms in their day to day discharge of duties and responsibilities. This ensures that goals of work units are achieved, and which in turn, creates inspirations towards achievements for the overall organizational performance. Through the implementation of Investors in People standards, LPU-B was able to create various innovations in terms of the way it manages its people. For example, the Investors in People requires that there should be a uniform leadership style being implemented all throughout the University. Thus, the Leadership Brand spelled in four C's (where every LPU leader should be: *Competent, Committed, Credible, and Caring)* was designed and introduced to all leaders in LPU. Each C has indicators that spell clearly the attributes that should be possessed by every LPU leader. Various orientations and training on how to implement the leadership brand were undertaken. Leaders are required to report at the start of the meeting on how they were able to implement the leadership brand for the past week. Later, the performance evaluation of every leader, and the teaching and non-teaching staff is being measured with reference to the Leadership Brand. The Leadership Brand allows leaders to continuously practice the standards not only of the Investors in People, but also the standards of other quality assurance tools. Additionally, the leaders are more empowered to create a sustainable transformational organization that promotes teamwork and unity among members.

Philippine Quality Award (PQA)

The Philippine Quality Award (PQA) is the highest level of national recognition for exemplary performance in the Philippines. This was established through Executive Order No. 448 by then President Fidel V. Ramos on October 1997. The award is given to organizations in the private and public sectors which excel in quality and productivity. The PQA requirements of the Criteria for Performance Excellence are embodied in seven categories namely: Leadership; Strategic Planning; Customer Focus; Measurement, Analysis, and Knowledge Management; Workforce Focus; Operations Focus; and Results (PQA Manual- 2012-2016). LPU-B applied for the PQA last May 31, 2012, and has been assessed by the PQA assessors last September 2012. LPU received the PQA recognition from President Benigno Aquino in a fitting ceremony held in Malacanang Palace last December 12, 2012. Through the PQA Malcolm Baldrige criteria, LPU-B is able to implement its standards of ADLI, which stands for Approach, Deployment, Learning and Integration. This means that for all strategies or approaches identified, there must be clear deployment, learning from the deployment, and integration of the learning that would surely promote outputs or results. This framework guided the LPU-B organizational members to focus not on processes alone, as required by the ISO 9001:2008 standards, but importantly on the outcomes or results of the processes. This way, organizational excellence that eventually promotes organizational transformation is evident to the LPU-B community.

Organizational Transformation

It can be said that the various quality assurance mechanisms being implemented in this University have gained several notable gains. This includes promotion of the quality programs and services that have brought laurels and recognitions to the organization. Some of these are the following: Top 2 in the Philippines with the highest number of PACUCOA accredited programs; Region's First Autonomous University with school wide ISO 9001:2008 certification; First HRM program in the Philippines to be Center of Excellence; First Tourism program in the Philippines to be Center of Development; First Investor in People Recognized University in the Philippines; Most Awarded HRM school in the Philippines- with 39 national championships and 3 international awards; First in the Philippines to have FULL accreditation in International Centre of Excellence (ICE) for Hotel and Restaurant Management and Tourism programs - this is along with other LPU schools in the Philippines (Manila, Cavite, Laguna);PQA "Recognition for Commitment to Quality Management" Recipient in 2012; Certified Home of Board Topnothers- over 231, and are still counting and over 65,000 graduates or alumni who now serve as agents of transformation in their respective communities.

A culture of strategic communication is another important factor in the strict observance of quality assurance mechanisms. In LPU-B, this is implemented through the creation of various advisory councils, such as: the management committee; the deans' council; the academic council; the administrative council and various ad hoc committees whose main task is to meet regularly to monitor day-to-day operations, as well as to identify policies and programs that would support the continuous improvements Through the periodic meetings and informal gatherings, the members of the organization have become committed to a culture of quality and excellence marked by a familiar spirit and a harmonious work environment. In LPU-B, the family culture is best exemplified by the openness of every LPU-B family member to change; one can say his opinion without having the fear of being discriminated or alienated. Aside from the warmth and friendliness of the work environment, there is also that sense of "malasakit" or entrepreneural spirit pervading in the whole organization. LPU-B greatest strengths are its people; they are able to express their individual styles and freely point out their ideas, yet they demonstrate group cohesion when it comes to achieving common goals such as delivering quality services or meeting or exceeding customer satisfaction.

Conclusions

More than these awards, quality assurance mechanisms undoubtedly fuel the passion in the hearts of organizational members to move towards higher levels of quality manifestations. As a members of one LPU-B family, they chart their future not only through the implementation of well tested management principles, embedded into our various quality assurance mechanisms, but importantly on the solid bedrock foundation of the belief that if all things are done out of pure love to quality, everything is possible. Organizational members have learned to recognize that it is only through their transformational attitude of deep love for quality that they can move LPU and themselves towards greater achievements. They have adopted the organizational learning that all team efforts should be dedicated to the University's dear Customers— the Students. This transformational attitude has acknowledged that the deep love for quality services can provide quality education to all graduates, who serve as agents of transformation of their respective communities. With this, in the LPU-B context, the essence of true transformation through quality assurance is: everyone in the organization serves g towards a common purpose that is aligned with the LPU-B mission: excellence in all things for God and Country PRO DEO ET PATRIA.

References

CMO #46 (2012). *Implementing Guidelines for CMO 46, s. 2012:* Policy Standard to enhance Quality Assurance (QA) in the Philippine Higher Education through Outcomes-Based & Typology Based QAP.

Investors in People (2012). *http://www.proveandimprove.org/new/tools/investors inpeople.php;* retrieved February 25, 2012.

Organizational Transformation (2014). *http://www.mbaskool.com/business-concepts. html,* retrieved November 26, 2014.

PQA (2012-2016). *Philippine Quality Award. Quest for Excellence. Criteria for Performance Excellence.*

Quality Assurance (2014). *BusinessDictionary.com,* retrieved November 19, 2014).

Ravhudzulo, N. A. (2012). Assessing best practice implementation of quality assurance in basic education by establishing standards and measuring program effectiveness. *Journal of Emerging Trends in Educational Research and Policy Studies, 3(4), 459*

Smith, Alan D. (2011). Quality assurance practices for competitive data warehouse management systems. *International Journal of Business Information Systems 7.4 Academic One File. Web.* 26 Nov. 2014.

15

Science and Technology Education in Nigeria for Reformation, National Values, Peace and Security

Patricia N. Eghagha

Abstract

*T*he paper examined science and technology education in Nigeria for reformation, national values, peace and security. It focused on the definitions of science and technology, it goals, reforms, peace education and security issues as it effects national values in Nigeria. Among the recommendations made were that government should take advantage of the provisions made by science and technology to improve on community security; agents should be trained and equipped by the government so that they can help on security issues at the grassroot level; more campaign and enlightenment on national values; peace and security should be created at grassroot level. Education International (EL) and UNESCO should not relent in their struggle to campaign for peace at all levels.*

Introduction

Education has remained a vital tool for rapid social, economic, political, scientific and technological development of any society. Science and technology are also agents for rapid social and societal development. There is no universal definition of science but it varies from one scientist to another. Some see science as 'what', 'How', and 'why' of things and happenings in the environment. Yet others see it generally as what scientists do. In more concrete terms, some scientists define science in term of its products or process. The products of science refer to the stock of accumulated knowledge stemming from the application of the processes (method) of science. Thus defined in terms of its products, science is an ordered body of knowledge in form of concepts, laws, theories, and generalization. The processes of science involve observing, classifying, measuring, experimenting, questioning, hypothesizing, recording, controlling variables, interpreting data, and communicating.

Technology, on the other hand, may be defined as the science of industrial arts. It is a systematic knowledge gained through science and its application to industrial processes. It is for most purposes regarded as applied science. Ogunniyi (1986) sees technology as the knowledge and study of human endeavors in creating or using tools, techniques, resources and systems to manage the man-made and natural environment for the purpose of extending human potentials and relationship of these to individual society and the civilization processes. Technology includes both physical objects and the techniques associated with them. It is the effective and efficient use of human and materials resources to produce goods and services. The method of technology usually represents the practical application of the theoretical understanding derived by science. Some of these factors include economic cost, aesthetic values, environmental, human utility and technical know-how. Science and technology education is therefore expected to give or provide support, by generating wide spread public understanding about reformation of any type, national values, peace and security. The adaptation of science and technology in national life marks the difference between development and under-development.

The Goals of Science and Technology Education

Science and technology education is closely linked with national development. The attainment of self-reliant and self-sustaining economy can only be achieved through technological development. The country is in dire need of industrialization and one of the vehicles to it is development of technology education.

The National Policy on Education (2004) revised stated the nature of science education to be achieved as follows:

> *Science education shall emphasize on the teaching and learning of science process and principle. This will lead to fundamental and applied research in the sciences at all levels of education.*

The goals of science education shall be:
- To cultivate inquiry, knowing and national mind for the conduct of a good life and democracy.
- To produce scientists for national development.
- Service studies in technology and the cause of technological development.
- To provide knowledge and understanding of the complexity of the physical world, the forms and the conduct of life.
- Special provisions and incentives shall be made for the study of the science at each level of the national education system. For this purpose, the functions of all agencies involved in the promotion of the study of science shall be adequately supported by Government.
- That Government shall popularize the study of science and the production of adequate number of scientists to inspire and support national development.

Science Education Reforms in Nigeria

Lots of reforms have taken place in science education in Nigeria. During the 1960's, a wide spread concern about science education started gathering momentum. The main complaint was that our curriculum in science was irrelevant to the world of work in which our children were brought up, thus, they pin-pointed gross imbalance, tremendous wastage and lack of proper articulation of our educational objectives

(Balogun, 1985). Perhaps, it was this crises, among other reasons, that motivated and provided the background for a new national policy on education, the 6-3-3-4 system of education whereby the two levels of education were broken into junior and senior secondary school, three years each, which necessitated the review of the o' level science syllabus.

A careful study of the policy shows that science education at the primary level is based on the objectives of primary education which is the laying of a sound basis for scientific and reflective thinking and the provision of opportunities for the child for developing manipulative skill that will enable him function effectively in the society within the limit of his capacity. This reform is to go further to ensure that the teaching methods to be employed de-emphasis the memorization and regurgitation of facts, encourage exploratory as well as experimental methods.

At the secondary school, more reforms have taken place using the broad aims of secondary education as its base stated briefly; the broad aims of secondary education in Nigeria are preparation for useful living within the society and preparation for higher education.

On adopting the National Policy on Education, science subjects were grouped as core subjects and subjects like wood-work, metal work, electronics, mechanics, home economics were grouped as prevocational subjects at the junior secondary school level. The core science subjects are taught to enable students offer science in higher education. On university education, a greater proportion of expenditure shall be devoted to science and technology education. Not less than 60% of places shall be allocated to science and science oriented course in the conventional universities. Not less than 80% in the universities of technology (National Policy on education, 2004).

Basic Education

The successive civilian governments also initiated a number of reform programs in virtually all sectors of the economy including education. So, in May 2004, by an act of the National Assembly, the Universal Basic Education (UBE) programme came into being. It shall be of 9 years duration comprising 6 years primary education and 3 years of junior secondary education. It shall be free and compulsory. It shall also include adult and non-formal education programmes at primary and junior secondary education levels for the adults and out of school youths. The specific goals of basic education shall be the same as the goals of the levels of education to which it applies (i.e. primary education, junior secondary education, adult and non-formal education).

The UBE as a reform programme has many basic features among are:

- Emphasis on curriculum diversification and relevance to effectively and adequately cover individual and community needs and aspirations;
- Individualized teaching methods;
- Introduction of rudiments of computer literacy;
- Appropriate continuous teacher professional development etc.

(Kpangban 2007)
Popularizing Science and Technology Education in Nigeria

Okoye (1997) stated that successive governments realizing the importance of science and technology education have done a lot to popularize science and technology in Nigeria. Among the many steps already taken were:

- The introduction of science fairs and science clubs in school. In the larger society there are trade fairs where new products arising from the application of new technologies are displayed.
- The introduction of junior engineer's technician's scientist (JETS) competition in secondary schools.
- The establishment of special science secondary school in some states of the federation.
- The pegging of the approved quota for admission into Nigerian Universities at sixty percent(60%) per science and science related subjects and forty percent (40%) for Arts;
- The establishment of specialized institutions in the areas of science and technology by the Federal Government e.g. (a.) Federal Universities of Technology (b.) Federal Universities of Agriculture.
- Award of scholarships to students studying science (including science related) and technology subjects.
- Establishment of polytechnics, technical colleges and colleges of education (technical) in many states of Nigeria;
- Organization of regular annual in service and short-term training to enhance the competence of science, mathematics and primary school teachers across the country.

A Combination of these efforts and investment has gone a long way in promoting the growth of science and technology education in Nigeria.

Science and Technology Curriculum Innovation in Nigeria

According to Uduogie (1997) science and technology education has under gone strain and stresses in Nigeria. The cooperative arrangement between the science teachers association of Nigeria (STAN) and the defunct Comparative Education Study and Adaptation Centre (CESAC) now merged into the Nigerian Education Research and Development Council (NERDC) heralded the national effort at science curriculum development to improved science education in Nigeria in 1968. Consequently, two major projects, the Nigerian Integrated Science Project (NISP) and the Nigeria Secondary School Science Project (NSSP) emerged. Later, the National Project Science and Mathematics Project (NPSMP) was developed. Thus an important sector of the education system-the primary and secondary schools was provided for. The innovation introduced centered on the integration of theory and practical in the student activities based science curricula for schools.

According to Federico (2000), the then UNESCO Director General, "Education International is not only a vast repository of experience, it also has the know-how and talent to implement innovation and change far beyond what is normally found in government circles. Education International (EL) and UNESCO can work together to achieve the common goals of an educated, intellectually curious and participatory culture of peace and democracy ". And that is also the position of science and technology education in Nigeria.

The educational action for promoting the concept of peace is concerned with the contest of education and training, educational resources and material, schools and university life, initial and ongoing training for teachers, research, and ongoing training for young people and adults. A culture of peace must take root in the class room from an early age. It must continue to be reflected in the curricula at secondary and tertiary levels. However, the skills from peace and non-violence can only be learned and perfected through practice, active listening, dialogue, medication and co-operation learning are delicate skills to develop. This is education in the widest sense. It is a dynamic, long term process: a life-time experience. It means providing both children and adults with an understanding of and respect for universal values and rights. It requires participation at all levels- family, schools, place of work, news-rooms, play ground and the community as well as the nation.

In the year 2000, Education International (EI) and UNESCO joined forces to produce a grassroot campaign for a culture of peace. The peace initiative was a sustained effort by EI to invite all its affiliates to join in the culture of peace. The kit outlined aspects of EI's ongoing commitment with human right and a peace culture from an education and union perspective. Curriculum development influenced by educational happenings in other lands which spread through mass media, tourism, studying abroad, journals, professional organizations, academic exchange programmes, explosion in information technology etc. have made significant changes in the curriculum in recent years.

New untraditional approaches in teaching secondary school science have emerged and more are being developed in all areas of science. Apart from these advantages, science and technology education in Nigeria have also contributed significantly to social and societal problems. Some of these problems are increase in crime, removal of natural resources without replacement, environmental pollution, treat to freedom, nuclear warfare etc. all these give rise to insecurity.

Therefore, Aliyu (2012) stated that while some people see national security in terms of a nation's military capacities or the struggle to overcome internal and external aggression, others consider a nation as secured once it is free from military threats or political coercion. The issues that constitute security threats also vary across nations. Whereas the major security threats to some powerful nations like the USA and its allies today may be how to defeat international terrorism and to promote their economic interest and democratic values, the developing countries like Nigeria may have their peculiar security challenges determined by our socio-economic and political circumstances.

In our own context, therefore, we may consider national security not only as the physical protection and defense of our citizens and our territorial integrity of which it is a part, but also the promotion of the economic well being and prosperity of Nigerians in a safe and secure environment that promote the attainment of our national interests and those of our foreign partners. While national security is intertwined with national interest, which is the pursuit of high standard of living for Nigerians, the promotion and protection of our core values, our dignity, our pride as Nigerians and our fundamental rights, as well as the entrenchment of social justice to engender peace, unity and development in our nation.

In essence, the concepts of economic prosperity, peace and social justice are germane to our contextual understanding of national security in Nigeria, for without economic stability and social justice at individual and societal levels, there will not be sustainable peace and national security will be undermined. Therefore, security is not an end in itself, but a critical means to the realization of national interest and aspirations. Hence we are all bound by the provision of the Nigeria constitution, which states in section 14 subsection (2)(b) that: "The security and welfare of people shall be the primary purpose of government".

Conclusions

This paper has dispassionately discussed the essence of education as a tool for National Development. Definitions of science and technology education, its goals, reforms, peace education, and security issues in Nigeria have also been streamlined. Therefore, without advanced knowledge in science and technology education, the issue of reformation, national values, peace and security will not be easily attained in Nigeria. To this end, educational system should be reformed with current knowledge in science and technology education and integrated into teaching and learning.

Recommendations

Based on the foregoing, the following recommendations are suggested:

- Government of Nigeria should take advantage of the provisions made by science and technology to improve on security.
- Community security agents should be trained and equipped by the government so that they can help on security issues at the grassroot level.
- Education International (EI) and UNESCO should not relent in their struggle to campaign for peace at grass-root level.
- NERDC should continue their good works in improving science education in Nigeria, while government should increase its commitment by funding NERDC.
- More campaign and enlightenment on national values, peace and security should be created at grass-root level.

Dr. Princewill Egwuasi

References

Aliyu, B. M. (2012). *The Search for National Security in Nigeria: Challenges and prospects.* Obafemi Awolowo Institute of Government and Public Policy, Agip Recital Hall, Muson, Lagos.

Balogun, T. A. (1985). Interests in science and technology Education in Nigeria. J.*STAN vol. 23: Nos. 1 and 2, pp 92-94*

Federico, M. (2000). *Education international.* United Nations Educational, Scientific and Cultural Organization (UNESCO).

Kpangban, E. (2007). *"The state of Education in Nigeria".*

National Policy on Education (2004). Federal Ministry of Education, Lagos.

Nigeria law (1999). *Constitution of the Federal Republic of Nigeria.*

Okoye, N. S. (1997). "Science and technology Education in Nigeria (ed.) by Gani A.B. and L.O. Ocho in *SMT Education in Nigeria.*

Ogunniyi, M. B. (1986). *Teaching science in Africa.* Ibadan: Sale Media

Udnogie, M. O. (1997). Science Education in Nigeria (ed.) by Gani and L.O Ocho in *SMT Education in Nigeria*

16

The Making of an Outcomes-Based Philippine Higher Education

Jake M. Laguador *PhD*

Introduction

Educational reforms and transformation in the curriculum of basic and higher education are some of the major challenges being faced by the Philippine Education System. The paradigm shift is now making its way to the full implementation of original plans and considering alternatives after doing rigorous observation based on experience. Outcomes-based education as a new approach towards the attainment of holistic individual and graduates in tertiary education is now taking its place in colleges and universities in the Philippines, to develop life-long learners who would possess the characteristics of being competent professionals ready to take leadership responsibilities in the diverse corporate world of business which is now getting smaller for competitions with the internationalization of education as the moving trend in the battlefield of ASEAN countries.

Implementation of Outcomes-Based Education (OBE) is the main thrust of most Higher Education Institutions in the Philippines today to go along with the standards of foreign universities and colleges all over the world (Laguador & Dotong, 2014). The primary aim of OBE is to facilitate desired changes within the learners, by increasing knowledge, developing skills and/or positively influencing attitudes, values and judgment. OBE embodies the idea that the best way to learn is to first determine what needs to be achieved. Once the end goal (product or outcome) has been determined, the strategies, processes, techniques, and other ways and means can be put into place to achieve the goal (Butler, 2004).

In the Philippines during 2007 and 2008, the Commission on Higher Education, through the efforts and recommendation of the Technical Panel for Engineering and Technology (TPET), has released a series of memoranda for compliance by all engineering schools offering baccalaureate engineering programs. The CHED Memorandum Order (CMO) mandated engineering schools to follow a new set of policies, standards and guidelines for all baccalaureate engineering programs that defined the needed competencies for the practice of each engineering field, and a set of program outcomes that engineering students in the different fields are expected to possess by the time they graduate. The first batch of students covered by these CMOs was expected to graduate in 2013 (CMO No. 77, s.2012).

In addition, according to CMO No. 46, series 2012, Section 13 states that:

> *"CHED is committed to developing competency-based learning standards that comply with existing international standards when applicable (e.g. outcomes-based education for fields like engineering and maritime education) to achieve quality and enable a more effective integration of the intellectual discipline, ethos and values associated with liberal education."*

The program outcomes common to all disciplines and types of schools may very well reflect some of the attributes of the HEI's ideal graduate, namely, the ability to: a) articulate and discuss the latest developments in the specific field of practice; b) effectively communicate orally and in writing using both English and Filipino; c) work effectively and independently in multi-disciplinary and multi-cultural teams d) act in recognition of professional, social, and ethical responsibility; e) preserve and promote "Filipino historical and cultural heritage (CHED Handbook on Typology, OBE, and ISA, 2014).

The HEI's vision and mission is an important aspect in the formulation of institutional goals and objectives which can be measured from the program outcomes. It defines the quality of graduates that the university produces overtime who contribute in the community development. Therefore, every academic institution has its own set of outcomes based on their goals and core values that they want to possess of their graduates.

Teaching and Learning Process

Teaching remains as the noblest profession, not only because it was introduced by Jesus Christ through His way of life, but also because man himself serves as the ultimate beneficiary and output of the said profession (Fajardo, 2014). Teaching and learning are processes which cannot be separated from one another. The development of learners through application of knowledge is an important aspect of outcomes-based education. Professionalization of teaching requires teachers and teacher educators to be involved in a learning process throughout their entire professional life (Tawanaand & Nkhwalume, 2013). Therefore, HEIs are now strengthening not the quality of instruction but the quality of learning.

Outcome-based education is a model of education that deviates from the traditional method of teaching which focuses on what the school provides to students but instead directs towards making students demonstrate that they "know and are able to do" whatever the required outcomes are (Reyes, 2013).

But still, teachers are always in the forefront of the most important and key services rendered by the university. In OBE, teachers serve as facilitators of learning. Keeping them abreast with the latest innovations and pedagogies in teaching would provide better learning atmosphere in classroom setting. Morales (2014) emphasized the integration of technology in the curriculum and instruction which would bring about significant student achievement leading to deep understanding of concepts for probable positive impact on student learning and achievement. Applying educational technology in the delivery of instruction would provide interactive better understanding of abstract concepts and simulation of processes which cannot be demonstrated through pure lectures without an aid of electronic devices or equipment.

Every teaching personnel must be very particular and sensitive to the needs of the students. Making the students feel satisfied to all the services being given to them is an enormous achievement for the university because it is a mark of commitment to quality education (Laguador, 2013). Teachers have an integral role in honing the abilities of the students. Their actions are consciously and unconsciously affecting the attitude of the students (Britiller et. al., 2014).

In recent educational development, the reinforcement of teaching through a diagnostic test has served as a tool to measure students' performance, which leads to enhancing or reminding students to have a good performance. This has been very useful for classroom teachers because it may give them satisfaction and confidence to work with the students (Elis, 2013).

English has been adopted as an official language of communication, a medium of instruction, has developed into a lingua franca in this country although it is not the Filipinos' mother tongue. Gathering and organizing information as study skills are counted as learning strategies that help augment the development of English proficiency (Haber, 2014). Everyone is encouraged to use English as a medium of communication and language for instruction to hone the confidence and skills of the learners in public speaking and technical writing which are essential part of the outcomes being measured by the OBE.

Research being one of the tri-focal functions of a university requires individuals capable enough in producing quality researches that would substantiate academic achievement and excellence (Abarquez & Palbacal, 2013). Conducting relevant researches as part of the culminating activity of each course provides a strong evidence of OBE (Laguador & Dotong, 2014).

The pedagogical philosophy is the lens through which the learning environment is seen. The courses in the curriculum and their mode of delivery should contribute towards the achievement of program outcomes. Non-academic programs should develop other qualities and values to complement the academic programs. Learning resources and support structures enable and enhance the teaching-learning systems. Program assessment should improve the learning environment. The other details will follow if the major features are clear to everyone. The learning environment should, therefore, be designed to produce the kind of ideal graduate of the HEI (CHED Handbook on Typology, OBE, and ISA, 2014).

Readiness and Resources

School administrators are still on the lookout of how they can maximize effectiveness of their utilization by enriching their resources and refining their skills to achieve a more effective teaching as well as functional learning (Fajardo, 2014).

With this trend, higher education is pressured to come up with quality assurance or quality enhancement of teaching and learning (Guico & Dolor, 2013). New and emerging technologies challenge the traditional process of teaching and learning and the way things are managed and controlled through OBE (Macatangay, 2013). It also develops the courageous initiative to remind concerned administrators, proprietors and educational leaders to augment university provisions of teaching devices and materials in order to upgrade college instructors' teaching skills/practices in using multimedia-assisted instruction in English (Fajardo, 2014).

Series of consultation with the stakeholders are being held to ensure that the student-outcomes will merit the approval and demand of the industries. Revision of instructional materials and the manner of skills' assessment were already modified through the use of rubrics. Whether the method of teaching being used is traditional or outcome based education, the need to evaluate the effect of the methods used to the student achievement is still necessary (Camello, 2014). Making every single output of the learners is considered as important product of their achievement in a certain task or project.

The task of implementing OBE at Philippine HEIs is expected to be far from easy during the early stages. The adoption of OBE can become complex and challenging with problems, particularly the teaching and learning activities, in achieving the intended learning outcomes and during assessment tasks. The OBE curriculum may be new not only to instructors and professors but also to HEI administrators, students and other stakeholders. Effectiveness in implementing OBE, self-evaluation, assessment techniques, and learning standards can be buzzwords in educational arguments among HEI administrators, teachers and students. Upon implementation of OBE, key policy focus areas may possibly include: how effective OBE is in the higher education, how to measure the effectiveness of OBE, and how to achieve the success indicators of OBE (Castillo, 2014).

In Lyceum of the Philippines University-Batangas (LPU-B), OBE started in 2011 to become part of the discussions in forums and convention. The University, like many other universities in Asia, deals with rapid and continuous challenges brought about by technological advancements and global demands. Javier (2012) stated that as an educational institution, it has to deliver the products and services necessary to achieve the outcomes it intends to produce.

As OBE practice in the LPU-B, students are required to keep all the exams, activities, and assignments in a portfolio for analysis by using a monitoring sheet (Brosoto, et al, 2014). With this requirement, OBE ensures a more objective assessment and fair result of predetermined criteria where students are being given proper orientations of OBE implementation. This is one way of ensuring that students are informed of their academic performance. Students were also being assessed through various examinations to measure the attainment of specific student outcome. Remedial classes and other intervention measures are being done to the students who obtained failing remarks in the assessment. The University maximizes the talents of the students through allowing them to utilize their skills in photography for the marketing purposes of the university, allowing the students to participate in conducting field researches, giving them the opportunity to represent the university in various competitions and research presentations.

Most universities in the country are already undertaking some of the educational practices involved in OBE. What they really need now is proper documentation of evidence of assessments and evaluation on the effectiveness of the program educational objectives after 4 or 5 years of graduation which will prove that the graduates are really equipped with essential knowledge, values (behaviour) and skills that can contribute to the development of the community.

References

Abarquez, R. R., Palbacal, J. A. (2013). Research Capabilities of International Tourism and Hospitality Management Faculty Members. *Journal of International Academic Research for Multidisciplinary, 1(7): 185-194*

Britiller, M. C., Ramirez, L. Q., Ramos, F. M. C., Reyes, D. M. C., Salazar, K. D., Sandoval, J. A. M. (2014). Nurse Educator's Affective Teaching Strategies. *Asia Pacific Journal of Multidisciplinary Research*, 2(1)

Borsoto, L. D., Lescano, J. D., Maquimot, N. I., Santorce, M. J. N., Simbulan, A. F., Pagcaliwagan, A. M. (2014). Status of Implementation and Usefulness of Outcomes-Based Education in the Engineering Department of an Asian University. *International Journal of Multidisciplinary Academic Research, 2(4), 2014*

Butler, M. (2004). Outcomes Based/ Outcomes Focused Education Overview. Retrieved from *http://www.kfshrc.edu.sa/saudization/files/Outcomes%20Based%20 Education.doc*. date retrieved: November 27, 2014

Camello, N. C. (2014). Factors Affecting the Engineering Students' Performance in the OBE Assessment Examination in Mathematics. *International Journal of Academic Research in Progressive Education and Development, 3(2), 87-103*

Castillo, R. C. (2014). A Paradigm Shift to Outcomes-Based Higher Education: Policies, Principles and Preparations. *International Journal of Sciences: Basic and Applied Research, 14(1), 174-186*

CMO No. 46, series 2012, *Policy-Standard to Enhance Quality Assurance (QA) in Philippine Higher Education through an Outcomes-Based and Typology-Based QA*, Section 13, p. 4.

CHED MEMORANDUM ORDER (CMO), No. 77, Series of 2012, "Policies, Standards and Guidelines in the Establishment of an Outcomes-Based Education (OBE) System in Higher Education Institutions Offering Engineering Programs".

Elis, J. C. (2013). Diagnostic Test in College Algebra for Freshman Non-Education Students of Westmead International School: Input to Proposed Remedial Activities. *Asia Pacific Journal of Multidisciplinary Research*, 1(1)

Fajardo, A. C. B. (2014). Multimedia-Assisted Instruction in Developing the English Language Skills: CBSUA Experience. *Asia Pacific Journal of Multidisciplinary Research, 2(2), 124-129*

Guico, T.M., Dolor, G. (2013). Level of Awareness and Possible Concerns of the Marine Faculty Members on Outcomes-Based Education. *Journal of International Academic Research for Multidisciplinary, 1(7): 159-167*

Haber, C. C. (2014). Learning Strategies Used by College Freshmen in Developing English Proficiency. *Asia Pacific Journal of Multidisciplinary Research, 2(2), 108- 114*

Handbook on Typology, Outcomes-Based Education, and Institutional Sustainability Assessment (2014), Commission on Higher Education, Philippines.

Javier, F. V. (2012). Assessing an Asian University's Organizational Effectiveness Using the Malcolm Baldridge Model. *Asian Journal of Business and Governance, 2: 37-55.*

Laguador, J.M. (2013). Developing Students' Attitude Leading Towards a Life-Changing Career, *Educational Research International*, 1(3): 28-33

Laguador, J. M. & Dotong, C. I. (2014). Knowledge versus Practice on the Outcomes-Based Education Implementation of the Engineering Faculty Members in LPU. *International Journal of Academic Research in Progressive Education and Development, 3(1), 63-74*

Macatangay, L. (2013). Tracer Study of BSCS Graduates of Lyceum of the Philippines University from 2004-2009. *Academic Research International, 4(5): 361-377*

Reyes, P. B. (2013). Implementation of a Proposed Model of a Constructivist Teaching-Learning Process – A Step towards an Outcome Based Education in Chemistry Laboratory Instruction. *Asia Pacific Journal of Multidisciplinary Research*, 1(1)

Tawanaand, L., Nkhwalume, A. A. (2013). In-service Mathematics and Chemistry Teachers' Preparednessfor Mathematics and Chemistry Courses at the University of Botswana: Issues and Challenges. *Asia Pacific Journal of Multidisciplinary Research*, 1(1)

HEALTH AND SAFETY ISSUES

17

Healthful School Environment

Joy-Telu Hamilton-Ekeke *PhD*

Abstract

*T*he health and even survival of human beings depend on their ability to adjust to their environment. Environmental health refers to the study of the factors in the physical environment which can influence human health while healthful school environment is more encompassing of all the things in the school environment (physical, social, biological and mental/emotional) that promotes pupils' as well as teachers' health. The school environment in which a child stays and learns determines to a large extent the effectiveness of learning and academic achievement in that individual. Healthful school environmental factors are required for safety, healthy living conditions and mental development for student academic excellence. School planning, organization and management are directly or indirectly related to healthful school environmental factors. A healthful school environment can improve health and increase students' and teachers' productivity while unhealthful school environment poses danger, insecurity, causes or intensifies illness among teachers and students which will result in high rate of absenteeism, less time in the classroom and ultimately reduced academic achievement. The school environment at nursery (pre-primary) to tertiary levels of education can be stimulating, interesting, pleasant, conducive to teaching-learning process or otherwise, depending on several factors like school rules against unhygienic conditions, the location of the school, the philosophy of the school, government policies and the cooperation or otherwise of the parents, teachers and the learners. This article thus discusses the various constituents of a healthful school environment.*

Introduction

Environment is a collective term used to describe all living and non-living things that make up a surrounding. Environment therefore consists of three components: physical environment, biological environment and social environment. The physical environment consists of all the non-living things in the surrounding such as air, water, climate, soil, house etc. the biological environment comprises all the living things in the surrounding such as animals, plants, man, microbes, etc., on the other hand, the social environment is made up of all the man-made materials such as culture, beliefs, religious practices, etc.

Healthful school environment is part of school health programme which also include health education and school health services, which are aimed at protecting and maintaining the health status of school children. According to Ogundele (2001), healthful school environment connotes the various physical, emotional and social aspects of the school and the measures provided at the school to ensure the health and safety of the pupils and school personnel. Most schools in Nigeria are in deplorable conditions without sound environmental health policies and the government fails to make appropriate fund available to promote maintenance of the school environment (Moronkola, 2012).

The Federal Ministry of Education (2006) stated that the school health programme comprises all projects or activities in the school environment for the promotion of the health and development of the school community. The main goal of school health programme in the Nigeria's National School Health Policy of 2006 is to improve the health of learners and staffs as responsible and productive citizens. The objectives of the school health programme as contained in Moronkola (2012) are:

- Promote growth and development of every child, taking into consideration his/her health needs;
- Create an awareness of the collaborative efforts of the school, home and the community in health promotion;
- Develop health consciousness among the learners;
- Create an awareness on the availability and utilization of various health-related resources in the community;
- Promote collaboration in a world of interdependence, social interaction and technological exposure in addressing emergent health issues;
- Build the skills of learners and staffs for health promotion in the community.

Healthful school environment as a subsidiary of the school health programme emphasizes the provision of healthful living environment in the school community that favours effective teaching-learning process. It concerns itself with the protection and improvement of conditions of the school environment, which influences students in one way or the other, especially the conditions of the building (light, air, sanitation and seating arrangement, teacher-pupil, teacher-teacher, pupil-pupil relationship and school lunch or meal programmes). Moronkola (2012) cited Ekeh (1978) that 'Healthful school environment cannot be isolated from the education of the child with regard to performance in the school'. The school's responsibility in the area of healthful environment is the provision of a safe and a healthful school environment, the organization of a healthful school day, the establishment of interpersonal relationships, favourable to emotional, social and physical health (Udoh, 1999). School environment in this paper will be discussed under the following headings below; how the factors under them affect pupils and school personnel's (academic and non-academic staffs) health:

- Physical Environment
- Biological Environment
- Social Environment
- Mental/Emotional Environment

Physical Environment

The physical healthful school environment includes all the external conditions or factors required in a healthy school environment for effective learning, its adequacy and availability determines positive learning and self-motivation among students (Anyanwu, Okpeze and Okpeze, 2012). The physical environment of a school should be safe, healthy and attractive as to motivate students in learning health. Udoh (2001) submitted that school, if well sited, is expected to be located on a reasonably well drained level ground, away from potential environmental hazards, and such school should also be accessible but reasonably isolated from the tick of housing area, busy highway, industrial plants, railroads, streams, ponds or be protected from hazards and trespasses by a suitable fencing with other essential amenities being provided.

The architectural design of school buildings, be it classrooms, laboratories, assembly halls or halls of residence, should be in line with the climate of the area and government approved master plan. The seating arrangement in classrooms should allow for easy movement and emergencies. School buildings needed to be accessible to both able and differently able school children and staff with access like stair cases as well as ramp respectively. There should be proper, and adequate ventilation, lighting, whether artificial or natural, it should be available except not needed. School buildings should be sited where there is low traffic and less noise, away from places like airports, markets, industries/factories, mosques and churches. This is to minimize outdoor noise and pollution.

Provision of safe and adequate water for drinking, laboratory, agricultural purposes and for other domestic use should be present in a school. The source of water should be known and supervised regularly to avoid water borne diseases and poisoning. Also many schools seem not ready or do not know how to manage its sewage (sewage primarily means liquid wastes emanating from domestic industrial and commercial effluents) and its refuse disposal (solid wastes are unwanted, discarded non-liquid materials emanating from various activities of human beings at home, school, industries etc., which may be combustible or non-combustible) system with the challenges of poor drainage and common erosion in some schools, the matter is worse. Schools should be inviting to students and staffs through its physical, social and emotional components of schools if appropriate teaching-learning tasks are to be done. It will be good to appreciate that a lot of time is spent each day in schools by students and staff. For school children, their future on diverse issues of life to a large extent depends on the environment of the schools they attend. Anderson and Creswell (1980) wrote that:

Some children come from homes with a high level of healthful living. This standard should further be fortified by a high level of healthful living in the school. When a child has grown up respecting healthful family and good living conditions, as an adult, he or she will likely maintain an excellent home life and insist on a wholesome community environment. From such preparation, community leaders develop respect for high standards which are the requisite of model citizen. For children whose life from the standpoint of healthful living is on a lesser plane, the school can serve both as an incentive in attaining a higher standard of healthful living. From school experience, many persons have established good living habits in their homes.

Biological Environment

Biological Environment entails all the living components of the school surrounding which include trees and flowers planted in the school, animals like dogs and other domestic pets and the unseen microbes in and around the school. Some of the objectives of school health services include: (i) Promote healthful growth both mentally and physically among school children; (ii) To instill principles of good healthful living in the school children and members of staff of the school through the examples of health personnel, demonstration and health education; (iii) To prevent occurrence of and spread of communicable diseases; (iv) To promote high level of sanitary condition in the school; (v) To provide individual or group counselling to pupils, parents and teachers; (vi) To provide emergency care for school children and if necessary their teachers; (vii) To provide screening services for early detection and treatment of defects; (viii) To ensure that the physical and social environment of the school is free from danger especially factors that can cause accidents.

Prevention and control of communicable diseases, according to Adetokunbo and Herbert (2000), is a legal responsibility of the health department, that is the Ministry of Health and its various units. It requires cooperation of nurses, medical and health related associations, school health educators, hospitals, industrial establishments, parents and other school personnel. In the same vein, Akinbile (1990) said that, four essential procedures are considered most useful in the control of communicability of diseases and according to WHO (2000), these are: (i) Health education (ii) Immunization (iii) Early detection of cases as well as treatment and or temporary exclusion of students from school and (v) environmental control measures, that is, the blocking of the routes of spread of diseases at school. This was seen implemented during the outbreak of ebola in Nigeria (June – September, 2014), where the resumption date of schools was postponed indefinitely to curtail the spread of the deadly virus amongst school children. Schools were allowed to re-open after Nigeria has been cleared by the World Health Organisation as 'ebola free'.

Ideally, policy should be made on communicable diseases control in schools. Immunization, isolation of infected students and re-admission to school after a bout of communicable disease are essential elements to be considered in such policy. The policy should be made known to both parent/guardian and students. It should spell out the responsibilities of parents and that of the school as follows:

- Responsibilities of parents include the observation of signs and symptoms of communicable diseases on their wards. They should also keep their wards at home to seek medical attention;
- Infected students should be excluded from school so that parents can take direct responsibility for their care;
- Readmission to school should be allowed as soon as the student recovers from illness and after such student has been certified that he or she constitutes no danger to other students or school personnel;
- Students on admission should be required to provide evidence of immunization against the killer diseases, which include: poliomyelitis, diphtheria, measles, whooping cough, tetanus and viral hepatitis. In like manner, school health educator helps in identification of diseases, provision of first aid, interpretation, counselling, advocacy and referral.

The sanitary condition of a school environment is another aspect of biological environment of a school which plays a significant role in determining the health status of the students and staffs of the school. In developing world in which Nigeria is one, the major causes of morbidity, mortality and presence of some communicable diseases are associated mostly with poor sanitation. Poor environmental sanitation provides suitable condition for micro-organisms which are causative agents of deadly diseases to thrive. Most life threatening diseases are preventable in a sanitized environment (Ojo, 2012). Unfortunately, there are still schools in Nigeria whose environment constitutes serious threat not only to the students but also to the entire school community/workforce.

Nigerian Facts and Figures (2007) contained data which support the dismal picture of environmental sanitation; about fifty eight percent (58%)of Nigerian households have no access to potable water sources, while twenty five percent (28%) have no access to sanitary facilities. This alarming statistics is worse in schools; the percent of schools without water sources and sanitary facilities is worse than the statistics of household. This extrapolation could be true if judged from the fact that house (home) where people live and spend more time of a twenty-hours day time, will not have water and sanitary facilities let alone schools where only a few hours is spent will there be water and sanitary facilities. The annoying thing about this saga is that government owned schools which lack these amenities will have on paper that the schools have functional amenities. There might be provisions for toilets and pipe borne water but probably not fixed or fixed but not functional.

With regards to solid waste, Oyediran (2004) asserted that about 0.43kg/head of solid waste is generated in Nigeria daily and 87% of Nigerians use insanitary refuse disposal methods. Cases of food-water borne diseases such as typhoid, cholera and food poisoning have also been on the increase in recent years and that the current environmental sanitation in Nigeria is so because Nigerians have developed and are sustaining a culture of filth which is been transferred or replicated in the Nigerian schools.

Social Environment

Social Environment of a healthful school consist of all the culture, policies, rules and regulations, school philosophy (vision and mission statements) geared towards the fulfillment of the objectives of the school health programme outlined above. When the social environment is good, there would be less violent demonstration, absenteeism, cult activities, examination malpractice, sexual exploitation, various other forms of abuse, suspension and expulsions and other social vices. Since the school is designed to explore and expand the frontier of knowledge, the social environment in schools should give room for the development of wholesome personal positive self concept, healthy attitude and practices, as well as the social skills of the learners.

The Nigerian primary school system up till secondary school concerns itself with teaching and learning while at tertiary level, especially in the universities, research forms substantial part of the work of both academic staff and students. The staff and students should be motivated through the provision of appropriate inputs (teaching-learning materials, appropriate facilities, conducive learning environment, remuneration, etc. (Hamilton-Ekeke, 2012), so that effective teaching-learning process is not hindered. This is important because, for effective learning to take place, both the teacher and the learner must be psychologically ready to perform their task.

The dimension of student's behavioral problems in schools may not be unconnected with unfavourable school environment. The problem of cultism has been a major threat to peace in tertiary education in Nigeria from late 1990's upwards, which may not be unconnected with the fact that students live in overcrowded halls, learn in overcrowded classrooms, recreational facilities are either inadequate or poorly maintained, libraries are with poor stock of current books, and journals which do not promote reading culture, poor basic social amenities like electricity supply, water supply and school staff, strikes, all make learning environment uncomfortable.

Communication is an aspect of school social environment that cannot be ignored. It is an important factor in healthful school environment as it is a vital instrument in individual and school performances, as teachers, students, parents and all stakeholders in the educational system of a country often value people with good communication skills. The following points are worthy of note by school community members so that receiver gets message as the sender desires it:

- Using simple language (spoken and written) which the receiver must understand. Even in setting examination questions, most questions must be to the comprehension ability of the learners and few complex ones to develop creativity, synthesis or innate ability of the learners. On no account should any form of communication be misunderstood;

- Non-verbal communication means like dressing, hairdo, body language, etc must be in line with the school culture reflecting sound moral principles. Therefore, both staff and students must dress neatly, and as cultured members of the school community;
- Messages passed across to school community members must be timeless and without being misconstrued by all;
- Staff and students must note as important, the setting at which message is sent and received;
- For effective communication, staff and students must be conscious of their body language and that of those they communicate with;
- It is expedient to pre-determine the likely effect of message sent or pre-determine the likely reaction of the receiver to the message to be sent.

Mental/Emotional Environment

The emotional climate of the school should be one that promotes healthy interaction among school staff, students, school authority and parents. This means that there is need for opportunities for self-respect, self-esteem, proven integrity, loyalty to the school management, pride in the school, caring and cohesiveness. Both the classroom and outside classroom environment of a school should promote healthful living. Anderson and Creswell (1980) listed the following as attributes/characteristics of a healthful mental environment in school/classroom:

- The children are relaxed and are at ease;
- They feel that they are wanted and regarded highly by their teacher and classmates. Their age-mates become their peer group, and approval of their peer group becomes progressively more important to the extent that they may rate peer approval more important than parental approval;
- They have a high level of self esteem;
- They are challenged by the situation;
- They are confident they can succeed;
- They experience success;
- They receive adequate personal gratification from their success.

But for these to be accomplished, Anderson and Creswell also noted that the school has these responsibilities:

- Recognize and identify children who are differently-able and needing emotional adjustment and support;
- Provide all the experiences that will stimulate in them desirable behavior;
- Provide students with aesthetic experiences capable of developing an awareness of beauty in life and help them identify with cultural groups;

• Provide opportunities for the development of concepts of values and for practices in conduct arising from these concepts.

Conclusions

Millions of children are affected by problems of poor nutrition, infectious diseases, inadequate access to clean water and sanitation, violence, substance abuse and the increasing threat and burden of living with HIV/AIDS etc. Children and young people need to be equipped with the knowledge, attitudes, values and skills that will help them face these challenges and assist them in making healthy life-style choices as they grow. The school environments therefore need to re-enforce the health education delivered through the curriculum in schools. The school environments (physical, biological, social, mental/emotional) need to compliment the health knowledge acquired and not be at variance with one another.

Recommendations

It is therefore recommended that schools should have proper approval before citing and building any school; that school planners and state government should pay adequate attention to proper planning, considering future expansion and development before citing any school. Funds should also be provided for infrastructure and maintenance of the old and dilapidated schools to avoid collapse. There should be proper fencing, installation of electrical appliances with other learning facilities to sustain student interest in school environment. And essential amenities (pipe borne water, electricity, toilet facilities with adequate provisions for hand washing) should be made available in every school especially government owned schools where contractors involved in giving hick backs to corrupt government officials to paid off uncompleted contracts. Private schools are better off in this regards as owners of schools personally monitor and supervise contractors in the construction of their schools. Related health facilities like gym, swimming pool, volley ball court, football pitch etc should be put in place by concerned government and authorities so that learners can be used to such facilities and utilize same in the community. Schools should endeavour to enforce the rules of hygiene so that their learners can integrate personal and community cleanliness as lifestyle. Finally, schools should devise strategies of rewarding positive health behaviours to reinforce healthy lifestyles among the learners.

References

Adetokunbo, O. L. & Herbert, M. G. (2000). *Short Textbook of Public Health Medicine for the Tropics.* Ibadan: Heinemann Educational Books (Nigeria) Ltd

Akinbile, P. O. (1990). Better health for all. *Nigerian School Health Journal, 10 (1&2): 8*

Anderson, C. L. & Creswell, W. H. (1980). *School Health Practice (7ᵗʰ ed.)* St Louis: The C.V. Mosby Company

Anyanwu, C. F., Okpeze, V. E. & Okpeze, C. N. (2012). *Physical healthful school environmental factors as predictors of motivation to learning in selected public secondary schools in Anambra State.*

Federal Ministry of Health (2004). *National Training Manuals for Environmental Health Practitioners pp 64-65*

Hamilton-Ekeke, J-T (2012). Public secondary school management staff assessment of status of health observation, examination and medical history keeping in Yenagoa, Bayelsa State. *Nigerian School Health Journal, 24(1): 21-33*

Moronkola, O. A. (2012). *School Health Programme (2012) 2ⁿᵈ edition.* Ibadan: Royal People (Nigeria) Ltd.

Nigeria Facts and Figures (2007). *BBC News*

National School Health Policy (2006). *Federal Ministry of Education, Nigeria.*

Ogundele, B. O. (2002). School health education in Z. A. Ademuwagun, J. A. Ajala, E. A. Oke, O. A. Moronkola & A. S. Jegede (Eds) *Health Education and Promotion.* Ibadan: Royal People (Nigeria) Ltd

Ojedokun, I. M. & Mojoyinola, J. K. (2012). The roles of school health programme in promoting the school children's health status in Nigeria. *Nigerian School Health Journal, 24 (1): 99-110*

Ojo, R. A. (2012). Preventing poor environmental sanitation in schools in Oyo metropolis through skills-based health education. *Nigerian School Health Journal, 24(2): 29-36*

Udoh, C. O. (2001). *Health education and health promotion in Nigeria by the year 2010.* A Valedictory Lecture presented at the Faculty of Education, University of Ibadan, Ibadan

Udoh, C. O. (1999). *Teaching Health Education.* Lagos: Kitams Academic Industries Publishers

World Health Organisation (2000). Local Action: Creating Health Promoting Schools. *WHO series on school health, pp 15-21*

18

Emergence of Cultism and Prostitution in Nigerian Campuses: Any difference in the Colleges of Education in Nigeria?

Henry D. Katniyon *PhD*, Pewat Z. Duguryil *PhD* & Martha I. Bulus

Abstract

The study investigated whether or not cultism and prostitution exist in the campuses of colleges of education in Plateau state. The sample for the study comprised of 143 students from Federal College of Education Pankshin and College of Education Gindiri. The design for the study was a survey design. The instrument for the study was a 24 – item, 5 point likert - type scale questionnaire titled; Pre service teacher's perception of the prevalence of cultism and prostitution questionnaire (PTPPCPQ). The reliability of the instrument gave a Cronbach Alpha correlation coefficient 0.82. It was discovered that cultism and prostitution is common among COEs Pre- service teachers. However, they seem to have a wrong perception of what prostitution is. The study discovered that cultism had serious negative effects on academic performance of students engaged in it. It was recommended that conspicuous bill boards warning about the harmful effects of cultism and prostitution should be mounted in all COE campuses, moral education should be made compulsory in primary and secondary schools in the country, also, cultism and its consequences should be treated in the General Studies courses in all tertiary institutions in the country.

Introduction

The Oxford Advanced Learner's Dictionary defined cult as a small group of people who have extreme religious beliefs and who are not part of any established religion. Their activities are mostly secretive as such are at times called secret cult. Ogunade (2002) defined a secret cult as an enclosed organized association or group devoted to the same cause. It is an enclosed group having an exclusive sacred ideology and a series of rites centering on their sacred symbols. Secret cult is a terminology coined by a former Military Head of State- Ibrahim Babangida between 1983 -1984. Before this period, these gangs had always been referred to as fraternities. The members of a cult group, according to Ogunade (2002) commit themselves to oath and allegiance, which serve as their strong bond. These groups of people are always violent when defending their course.

There are many secret cults in Nigeria and they are not restricted to any particular place in the country. They are found among the various ethnic groups. They have been in existence since the pre-colonial period in Nigeria. Some of them have now been reformed. Ogunade (2002) categorized them into three groups: religious secret societies, semi-religious secret societies and anti-social secret societies.

Cultism has become a major social problem facing universities both within and outside the country. The problem of increasing violent cult and gang activities in Nigerian universities is of great concern to parents, school authorities and the nation at large. This is because of the heightened tensions, prevailing uncertainty, campus violence and fierce struggle for supremacy that has characterised the activities of cult groups of recent. Our news papers are replete with reports on the unprecedented severe violence from various cult groups in Nigerian universities.

Cultism found its way into the Nigerian institutions of learning as far back as early 50's (Oguntuase, 1999). The disruptive activities of cult groups in Nigerian universities which started in the late 80's may not be unrelated to loss of values in the society. Oguntuase (1999) reports that the first cult-related violent death occurred in 1984. A sentinel survey carried out on various tertiary education campuses and vicinities showed that between 1995 and 2004, about 1,743 cultists have died; about 23 innocent students became victims of circumstances. The report further reveals that about 6,733 cultists were maimed and about 115 innocent students sustained various degrees of injuries.

Another vice of concern on our campuses is prostitution. Prostitution on campus involves especially females engaging in pre- marital illicit sexual services or cohabitation with male partners in or outside the campus for educational or economic gains or both. The growing rate of campus prostitution in Nigerian tertiary institutions today is a thing of serious concern to all well meaning Nigerians. The tertiary institution is the last stage of moulding leaders of tomorrow which prepares them to be leaders and policy makers for the future; as such if our colleges are now saturated with the menace of prostitution and its control syndicate, then the nation is in deep crisis. Campus prostitution is now so common that the culprits do not hide their trades. This is a bad omen for motherhood and academic excellence. Prostitution has the tendency to debase motherhood and corrupt the social fabrics of the society which is likely to cripple the developmental effort of the country. This is because societies that are not armed with sound morals are not ruled by good leaders and do not deserve life of existence.

Unfortunately, politicians, lawmakers, businessmen and major office holders are the major patrons of these students. Ukpashi (2014) commented that a visit of female hostels at night will convince one of the dimensions that prostitution has taken. The flashy cars that come to pick these girls for one function or the other is a pointer to the fact that their sex partners are people that matter in society. The consequences of this situation are that girls no longer respect their lecturers or constituted authorities in their respective schools. Academic indiscipline has crept into the ivory towers, which is negatively affecting academic excellence and quality of graduates that are turned out every year. The values of character, hard work, research and intellectual pursuit, are being eroded as most of these students have already known that the only thing they need is to bribe the lecturers involved, both in kind and cash to get the required marks.

Cultism and prostitution have a lot of devastating effects on those that practice them. Some of the effects include:

1. Retardation of Individual Development

- It has brought premature death to many youthful lives.
- It affects the morale of the individual
- It promotes acts of indiscipline and immorality among youth.
- It renders the individual unsociable, psychologically deranged, emotionally destabilized mentally and spiritually confused.
- It exposes the individual to HIV/AIDS through mutual sharing of same unsterilized piercing object during initiation and the use of same unsterilized syringes and needles during drug abuse.
- After initiation, they assume 'Super-human' form, and indulge in criminal activities e.g. armed robbery, assassins, kidnappings, rape, assault and battery, drug peddling and others that can take them to jail, if found guilty.
- Most cultist cum gangsters are potential rapist, and research has revealed that most rapists hardly use condom during sex orgy or rape.
- The fortunate ones graduate to become half- baked graduates.

2. Retardation of Educational Development

- It erodes quality and standard of education.
- It diminishes integrity and confidence in our educational system.
- It creates an entrenched disincentive to academic pursuit and planning excellence.
- It threatens the peaceful and progressive co-existence in our campuses and vicinities.

3. Retardation of Societal and National Developments

- It has been a threat to the internal security of the nation leading to loss of lives and properties.
- It has brought untold sorrow to many homes whose wards had been killed, maimed, raped, expelled, rusticated or victimized.
- It weakens the family ties and societal cum cultural values due to its success in producing 'monsters' for the nation which has made them to be nuisance to themselves, eyesore to their families and a bunch of nonentities to the society.
- It tarnishes the country's already battered image, credibility and national pride.

With the fore mentioned effects, it is obvious that cultism and prostitution are canker worms that must be addressed headlong. Whether or not the ugly trend of this canker worm has permeated teacher training institutions at the colleges of education level is a question that beckons for an answer. Also, most of the works reported so far seem to point to the universities as the major breeding ground of cultists. There is therefore the need to investigate the situation at the colleges of education levels, which is what this study sets out to do. The study is guided by four research question.

Research questions

The following research questions were stated to guide the research:

- To what extent are colleges of education students involved in cultism?
- To what extent are colleges of education students involved in prostitution?
- What are the colleges of education students' perception of the effect of cultism on the academic performance of those engaged in it?
- What are the colleges of education students' perception of the effect of prostitution on the academic performance of those involved in it?

Methodology

The study investigates whether or not cultism and prostitution exist in the campuses of colleges of education in Plateau State. The population for the study comprised of students from Federal College of Education Pankshin and College of Education Gindiri. The design for the study was a survey design. 143 subjects were randomly selected from the population. The respondents comprised of 84 males and 59 females pre-service teachers.

Instrument

The instrument for the study was a 24 – item 5 point likert - type scale questionnaire titled; Pre service teachers' perception of prevalence of cultism and prostitution questionnaire. This was validated by experts in education and test & measurement. Using the Cronbach Alpha correlation coefficient, the reliability of the instrument was found to be 0.82.

Results

Research Question 1: To what extent are Colleges of education students involved in cultism?

Table 1: COE Students' Involvement in Cult Related Activities

S/N	Statements	Mean
1	I think there is cultism in my school.	3.83
2	Cultism is harmless.	3.08

3	Cult members only fight when is necessary.	2.73
4	I think some activities of cult members is good for my/our college.	3.53
5	I think cult members join armed robbery gangs.	4.02
6	There is cultism even in the secondary schools.	3.52

Data in Table 1 shows that the pre service teachers from the COEs agree that cultism is prevalent in their campuses with a mean value above 3.00 in all the items except item 3 with a mean of 2.73 which shows that students agree that cult members also fight even when it is not necessary.

Research Question 2: To what extent are COE students' involved in prostitution?

Table 2:   COE Students' Involvement in Prostitution Related Activities

S/N	Statements	Mean
1	I think the practice of campus couples is common in my school.	3.86
2	I think prostitutes stay only in hotels and brothels.	3.74
3	To me illicit sex is an expression of love and not prostitution.	3.73
4	I do not see a girl staying with her boyfriend as prostitution.	3.70
5	I think abortion is common among students in the college.	4.06
6	To me prostitution can lead to barrenness.	4.27

Responses from Table 2 show that in items 1, 4, and 5, respondents agree that there is prostitution on the campuses. Item 6 tend to agree that a negative effect of prostitution exist on female students. Whereas for items 2 and 3, respondents see indiscriminate sex as expression of love and see prostitutes as staying only in hotels and brothels.

Research Question 3: What is the COE students' perception of the effect of cultism on the academic performance of those engaged in it?

Table 3: COE Students' Perception of the effects of cultism on the performance of those involved in it

S/N	Statements	Mean
1	Cult members are often regular in class.	1.82
2	Cult members are often top of their classes.	1.05
3	Cult members often miss some test.	3.50
4	Cult members submit assignments late.	4.50
5	Cult members engage in exams malpractice.	3.24
6	Cult members harass teachers for marks.	3.34

Data in Table 3 shows that respondents perception of effect of cultism is that they are irregular in class with a mean of 1.82, do not top their class (mean, 1.05), miss test and submit assignment late (mean, 4.50) and harass teachers for marks (mean, 3.34).

Research Question 4: What is the COE students' perception of the effect of prostitution on the academic performance of those involved in it?

Table 4: COEs Students Perception of the Effects of Prostitution on Academic Performance of Those Involved in it.

S/N	Statements	Mean
1	To me prostitution can lead to barrenness.	4.27
2	Campus couples in my college are irregular in class.	4.10
3	Girls with multiple boyfriends often engage in examination malpractice.	3.50
4	Boys with multiple girlfriends often engage in examination malpractice.	4.03
5	Boys who engage as campus couples (cohabitation) do not do well in class.	3.70
6	Girls who engage as campus couples (cohabitation) do not do well in class.	3.95

Data in Table 4 reveals that prostitution-related activities have negative effects on COE students' performance. Items 2 and 6 show that respondents agree that students involved in campus cohabitation are irregular in class, have low performance and engage in vices such as examination malpractice as all have means above 3.00.

Discussion

The issue of cultism and prostitution seem to be on the rise in Nigeria today. From the study on the emergence of cultism and prostitution on our COE campuses, it was discovered that cultism and prostitution are common among COE Pre- service teachers. Cultism and ocultic practices started as far back as 1980s as observed by Oguntuase (1999). Studies revealed that most of the cult activities reported in the past in Nigeria occurred at the university campuses. This bad trend has extended its tentacles now to the COE campuses as observed by the Pre service teachers in this study. The mandate of COEs is to train teachers for the lower levels of education, if such students turn out to be cultists, then the effect on the younger generation could only be better imagined.

One of the research questions sought to find out whether students at COE campuses are engaged in prostitution. Findings revealed that some students are involved in prostitution. However, they seem to have a wrong perception of what prostitution is. This is because they do not see indiscriminate sex as prostitution but rather as an expression of love. They see prostitutes as staying only in hotels and brothels.

Google sites (2014) identified four types of prostitution which are streetwalker, child/ adolescent, home prostitute and call girls. From the study it was discovered that the type common to COE students is the home and streetwalker type of prostitution. This has serious health, moral and educational implications.

The study also sought to find out the effect of cultism on the academic performance of COE students. The study discovered that cultism had serious negative effects on academic performance of students engaged in it. For instance it was discovered that cult members were often engaged in examination malpractice and harassment of lecturers for marks. This position agrees with John (n. d.) who associated cultism to violent practices on campus which is a hindrance to the training of productive workforce for national development.

As to whether or not prostitution affects COE students' academic performance, it was discovered that prostitution had serious negative effects on the performance of students engaged in it. They were discovered to be irregular in class, perform poorly, and engaged in examination malpractice. Google sites (2014) ascribe poor academic performance and school drop out to prostitution related activities. Since the respondents did not have a clear perception of what prostitution is, there is the need to educate them on what prostitution is and its implication on their academic performance.

Conclusions

This study investigated whether cultism and prostitution exist on the campuses of Colleges of Education in Plateau State. It was discovered that the practices exist and are practiced in varying forms. Implications of these practices on students' academic performance, health and wellbeing were discussed. Also, students understanding regarding these practices were observed to be defective. It was recommended that students should be educated on how to avoid these practices.

Recommendations

Cultism is a social crime and the activities of cultists are sometimes laden with blood. Through the cultists' activities, many lives have been lost, many people maimed and many students have been rusticated. There is the urgent need to put an end to it. Some people have openly declared that cultism is as worst as armed robbery. So, in order to curb it, there should be:

- Conspicuous bill boards warning about the harmful effects of cultism and prostitution. This should be mounted in all COE campuses.
- Moral education should be made compulsory in primary and secondary schools in the country.
- Cultism and its consequences should be treated in the General Studies courses in all tertiary institutions in the country.

- Parents should take time to understand their children, give enough time to listen to them at home and satisfy their emotional, psychological and physical needs.
- Parents should watch the friends their wards are keeping in the institutions. Take time to watch any misbehavior put up by their wards and correct immediately..
- Aggressive campaign against cultism in all tertiary institutions should be mounted.

References

Google sites (2014). Prostitution. *http://sites.google.com/sites/prostitution Retrieved August 2013*

John, J. (n.d.). The menace of cultism in our institutions. An unpublished Pamplet.

Ogunade, R. (2002). Secret societies and-cultic activities in Nigerian tertiary institutions in *Leading Issues in-General Studies.* University of Ilorin Press.

Ogunlusi B. (2003). 'Awe Vs Soyinka." *The Guardian.,* June 23rd. *Sociology of Education, 2008.*

Oguntuase B. (1999). Cultism and violence in higher institution in Nigeria. A paper presented at the anti- cult week of University of Lagos, November, 3rd.

Ronald. E. (1980). Australia: Book House Australia Ltd.

Ukpashi E. (2014). The menace of prostitution in Nigerian tertiary institution *www. facebook.com/ukpashie1?* Retrieved/ September, 2013

Walter. R. M. (1970). *The kingdom of the cults.* Minnesota: Bethany fellowship inc.

19

Plant Tissue Culture in a Biological Environment

Helen N. Odiyoma

Introduction

Tissue culture is the growth of tissues or cells separate from the organism. This is typically facilitated through the use of liquid, semi-solid growth medium, such as broth or agar. Tissue culture commonly refers to the culture of animal cells and tissues, with the more specific term plant culture being used for plants.

In 1885, Wilhelm Roux removed a section of the medullar plate of an embryonic chicken and maintained it in a warm saline solution for several days, establishing the basic principle of tissue culture. In 1907, the zoologist Ross Granville Harrison demonstrated the growth of frog embryonic cells that would give rise to nerve cell in a medium of clotted lymp. In 1913, E. Steinhardt, C. Isreali and R.A Lambert grew vaccinia virus in fragment of guinea pig corneal tissue. In 1996, the first use of regenerative tissues were used to replace a small distance of a urethra, which led to the understanding that the technique of obtaining samples of tissue, growing it outside the body without a scaffold, and reapplying it, can be used for only small distance of less than 1cm.

In recent development, tissue culture generally refers to the growth of cells from a tissue from a multicellular organism in vitro. These cells may be cells isolated from a donor organism, primary cell, or an immortalized cell line. The cells are bathed in a culture medium, which contains essential nutrient and energy source necessary for the cells survival. The term tissue culture is often used interchangeable with cell culture. Literally, tissue culture refers to the culturing or growing of tissue pieces.

This is called explants culture. Tissue culture is an important tool for the study of the biology of cells from multicellular organisms. It provides an in vitro model of the tissue in a well defined environment which can be easily manipulated and analyzed.

Explant Culture

In Biology, explants culture of cord life group is a technique used for the isolation of cells from a piece or pieces of tissue. Tissue harvested in this manner is called explants. It can be a portion or the shoot, leaves or some cell from a plant, or can be any part of the tissue from an animal or umbilical cord tissue.

In summary, the tissue is harvested in an aseptic manner, often minced and pieces placed in cell culture dish containing growth medium. Over time, progenitor cells migrate out of tissue onto the surface of the dish. These primary cells then be further expanded and transferred into fresh dishes.

Explants culture also refers to the culturing of the tissue pieces themselves, where cells are left in their surrounding extra cellular matrix to move accurately mimic the in vitro environment.

Cell Culture

This is a complex process by which cells are grown under controlled conditions, generally outside of their natural environment. The term cell culture refers to the culturing of cells derived from multi-cellular eukaryotes, especially animals cells. However, there are also culture of plants, fungi, insect and microbes, including viruses, bacteria and protists. The historical development and methods of cell culture are closely interrelated to those of tissue culture and organ culture.

Cell culture has being applied in many ways, in the manufacture of viral vaccines and other product of biotechnology.

Biological products produced by recombinant DNA (rDNA) technology in animal cell cultures include enzymes, synthetic hormones, immunobiologicals (monoclonal antibodies, interleceukins, lymphocytes) and anticancer agents. It is expensive, to grow mammalian cell culture, so research is underway to produce such complex proteins in insect cell or in higher plants.

Plant Tissue Culture

This is a collection of techniques used to maintain or grow plant cells, tissues or organs under sterile condition on a nutrient culture medium of known composition. Plant tissue culture is widely used to produce clones of plants in a method known as micro propagation.

Different technique in plant tissue culture may offer certain advantage over traditional method of propagation, including:

- Production of exact copies of plant that produce particularly good flowers, fruits or have other desirable traits.
- It quickly produces mature plants.
- It produces multiples of plants in the absence of seeds or necessary pollinators to produce seeds.
- Regeneration of whole plants from plant cells that have been genetically modified.
- It cleanses particular plants of viral and other infections and quickly multiplies these plants as cleansed stock for horticulture and agriculture.
- Production of plants from seeds that otherwise have very low chances of germinating and growing. Examples here are Orchids and Nepenthes.

- Production of plants in sterile containers that allows them to be moved with greatly reduced chances of transmitting disease pests and pathogens.
- Plant tissue culture relies on the fact that many plant cells have the ability to regenerate a whole plant (totipotency).
- Single cells, plant cells without cell walls (protoplasts), pieces of leaves, stems or roots can often be used to generate a new plant on culture media given the required nutrients and plant hormones.

Hydroponics is a subset of hydroculture and is a method of growing plant using mineral nutrient solution or aqueous solutions, in water, without soil. Terrestrial plants may be grown with their roots in the mineral nutrient solution only or in an inert medium, such as perlite or gravel. Hydroponics had begun by the 1860s. This practice, along with the ability of plants to reproduce asexually led the German botanist Gottlieh Haberlandt to speculate in 1902 that entire plant could be produce by tissue culture. Tissue culture is the growth of a tissue in an artificial liquid or solid culture medium. Haberlandt said that plants cells are totipotenl.

Plant Tissue Culture Techniques

Modern plant tissue culture is performed under aseptic conditions under HEP A filtered air provided by a laminar flow cabinet. Living plant materials from the environment are naturally contaminated on their surfaces (and sometimes interiors) with microorganisms, so surface sterilization of starting material (explants) in chemical solutions (usually alcohol and sodium or calcium hypochlorite) is required. Explants are then usually placed on the surface of a solid culture medium, but are sometimes placed directly into a liquid medium, particularly when cell suspension cultures are desired. Solid and liquid media are generally composed of inorganic salts plus a few organic nutrients, vitamins and plant hormones. Solid media are prepared from liquid media with the addition of a gelling agent, usually purified agar. The composition of the medium, particularly the plant hormones and the nitrogen source have peofound effects on the morphology of the tissues that grow from the initial explant. For example, an excess of auxin will often result in a proliferation of roots, while an excess of cytokinin may yield shoots.

A balance of both auxin and cytokinin will often produce an unorganised growth of cells, or callus, but the morphology of the outgrowth will depend on the plant species as well as the medium composition. As cultures grow, pieces are typically sliced off and transferred to new media (subcultured) to allow for growth or to alter the morphology of the culture. The skill and experience of the tissue culturist are important in judging which pieces to culture and which to discard. As shoots emerge from a culture, they may be sliced off and rooted with auxin to produce plantlets which, when mature, can be transferred to potting soil for further growth in the greenhouse as normal plants.

Regeneration Pathways

The specific differences in the regeneration potential of different organs and explants have various explanations. The significant factors include differences in the stage of the cells in the cell cycle, the availability of or ability to transport endogenous growth regulators, and the metabolic capabilities of the cells. The most commonly used tissue explants are the meristematic ends of the plants like the stem tip, auxiliary bud tip and root tip. These tissues have high rates of cell division and either concentrate or produce required growth regulating substances including auxins and cytokinins. Shoot regeneration efficiency in tissue culture is usually a quantitative trait that often varies between plant species and within a plant species among subspecies varieties, cultivars, or ecotypes. Therefore, tissue culture regeneration can become complicated especially when many regeneration procedures have to be developed for different genotypes within the same species. The three common pathways of plant tissue in cultures regeneration are:

- Propagation from preexisting meristems (shoot culture or nodal culture)
- Organogenesis
- Non-zygotic (somatic) embryogenesis

The propagation of shoots or nodal segments is usually performed in our stages for mass production of plantlets through in vitro vegetative multiplication. Organogenesis is a common method of micro propagation that involves tissue regeneration of adventitious organs or axillary buds directly or indirectly from the explants. Non-zygotic embryogenesis is a noteworthy developmental pathway that is highly comparable to that of zygotic embryos and it is an important pathway for producing somaclonal variants, developing artificial seeds, and synthesizing metabolites. Due to the single cell origin of non-zygotic embryos, they are preferred in several regeneration systems for micropropagation, ploidy manipulation, gene transfer, and synthetic seed production. Nonetheless, tissue regeneration via organogenesis has also proved to be advantageous for studying regulatory mechanisms of plant development.

Choice of Explants

The tissue obtained from a plant to be cultured is called an explants. Based on work with certain plants, particularly tobacco, it has often been claimed that a toti potent explants can be taken from any part of a plant including portions of shoots, leaves, stems, flowers, roots and single, undifferentiated cells.. However this is not true for all plants.^ In many species explants of various organs vary in their rates of growth and regeneration, while some do not grow at all. The choice of explants material also determines if the plantlets developed via tissue culture are haploid or diploid. Also the risk of microbial contamination is increased with inappropriate explants.

The first method involving the meristems and induction of multiple shoots is the preferred method for the micropropagation industry since the risks of somaclonal variation (genetic variation induced in tissue culture) are minimal when compared to the other two methods. Somatic embryogenesis is a method that has the potential to be several times higher in multiplication rates and is amenable to handling in liquid culture systems like bioreactors.

Some explants, like the root tip, are hard to isolate and are contaminated with soil microflora that become problematic during the tissue culture process. Certain soil microflora can form tight associations with the root systems, or even grow within the root. Soil particles bound to roots are difficult to remove without injury to the roots that then allows microbial attack. This associated microflora will generally overgrow the tissue culture medium before there is significant growth of plant tissue.

Some cultured tissues are slow in their growth. For them there would be two options:

- Optimizing the culture medium;
- Culturing highly responsive tissues or varieties. Necrosis can spoil cultured tissues. Generally, plant varieties differ in susceptibility to tissue culture necrosis. Thus, by culturing highly responsive varieties (or tissues) it can be managed.

Aerial (above soil) explants are also rich in undesirable micro flora. However, they are more easily removed from the explants by gentle rinsing, and the remainder usually can be killed by surface sterilization. Most of the surface micro flora do not form tight associations with the plant tissue. Such associations can usually be found by visual inspection as a mosaic, de-colorization or localized necrosis on the surface of the explants.

An alternative for obtaining uncontaminated explants is to take explants from seedlings which are aseptically grown from surface-sterilized seeds. The hard surface of the seed is less permeable to penetration of harsh surface sterilizing agents, such as hypochlorite, so the acceptable conditions of sterilization used for seeds can be much more stringent than for vegetative tissues.

Tissue cultured plants are clones. If the original mother plant used to produce the first explants is susceptible to a pathogen or environmental condition, the entire crop would be susceptible to the same problem. Conversely, any positive traits would remain within the line also.

Applications

Plant tissue culture is used widely in the plant sciences, forestry, and in horticulture. Applications include:

- The commercial production of plants used as potting, landscape, and florist subjects, which uses meristem and shoot culture to produce large numbers of identical individuals.
- To conserve rare or endangered plant species.^
- A plant breeder may use tissue culture to screen cells rather than plants for advantageous characters, e.g. herbicide resistance/tolerance.
- Large-scale growth of plant cells in liquid culture in bioreactors for production of valuable compounds, like plant-derived secondary metabolites and recombinant proteins used as biopharmaceuticals.^
- To cross distantly related species by protoplast fusion and regeneration of the novel hybrid.
- To rapidly study the molecular basis for physiological, biochemical, and reproductive mechanisms in plants, for example in vitro selection for stress tolerant plants, and in vitro flowering studies.
- To cross-pollinate distantly related species and then tissue culture the resulting embryo which would otherwise normally die (Embryo Rescue)?
- For chromosome doubling and induction of polyploidy, for example doubled haploids, tetraploids, and other forms of polyploids. This is usually achieved by application of antimitotic agents such as colchicine or oryzalin.
- As a tissue for transformation, followed by either short-term testing of genetic constructs or regeneration of transgenic plants.
- Certain techniques such as meristem tip culture can be used to produce clean plant material from virused stock, such as potatoes and many species of soft fruit.
- Production of identical sterile hybrid species can be obtained.

Laboratories

Although some growers and nurseries have their own laboratories for propagating plants by the technique of tissue culture, a number of independent laboratories provide custom propagation services. The Plant Tissue Culture Information Exchange lists many commercial tissue culture laboratories. Since plant tissue culture is a very labour-intensive process, this would be an important factor in determining which plants would be commercially viable to propagate in a laboratory.

References

Aina, O., Queensberry, K. & Gallo, M. (2012), In Vitro induction of tetraploids in Arachis.

Chalk, L. (1050). *Anatomy of dicotyledons.* Vols. 2 Oxford clarendon press, pp. 1500

Dutta, A. C. (1970). Fifth edition. Madras: Oxford university press

Egho, E. O. (1995). *A New Approach Biology for senior secondary schools and colleges. Second edition.* Benin City: B. E. Publishers.

Egho, E. O. (2008). *A New Approach Biology for senior secondary schools and colleges. New edition.* Benin City: B. E. Publishers.

Madder, S. S. (2004). *Biology. Eight edition.* New York: McGraw-Hill Publishers.

Mclaren, R. (1985). *Heath Biology.* Canada: D. C. Heath and Company.

Bhojwani, S. S., & Razdan, M. K. (1990). *Plant tissue culture: Theory and Practice* (Revised ed). Elessvi.

Geeorgiev, M. I., Weber, J., & Mukluk, A. (2009). Bio processing of plants cell culture for mass production of targeted compounds. *Applied Microbiology and Biotechnology. 83(5) 809-23. Dio 10. 1007/500253-009-2049-x. PMID 19488748*

ENTREPRENEURSHIP ISSUE

20

Entrepreneurship Education and Students' Employment Generation in Niger Delta University Bayelsa State, Nigeria

Diepriye Okodoko *PhD*, Anderson P. Sele *PhD* & Ebitimi G. Bekebo

Abstract

*T*he primary purpose of the study was to examine entrepreneurship education and students' employment generation in Niger Delta University of Bayelsa State, Nigeria. The research design used in this study was the correlation survey design. The target population for this study was made up of all students' that took part in entrepreneurship education from four selected faculties in Niger Delta University of Bayelsa State. The total population was 1243. A sample size of 310 was used for the study which represented (25 percent) of the total population, which was selected through the proportionate stratified random sampling technique. An instrument tagged; "Entrepreneurship Education and Students' Employment Generation Questionnaire" (EESEGQ) was used to collect data for the study. Test–retest method with Pearson Product Moment Correlation coefficient (PPMC) was used to establish the reliability coefficient of the instrument which yielded 0.81. Two research questions and corresponding hypotheses were raised for the study. Data gathered in this study were analyzed with mean, standard deviation and Pearson Product Moment correlation coefficient. The results from the findings revealed that, there is a significant relationship between knowledge on fish farming and employment generation among students'. On the basis of the findings, it was concluded that, Knowledge on fish farming has a significant relationship with employment generation among students' in Niger Delta University of Bayelsa State. The researchers' therefore made some recommendations among which are that; Students' should acquire more knowledge on fish farming so that their self employment generation opportunities could be created.*

Introduction

The importance of entrepreneurship education to the development of the economy has been the subject of increased attention in Nigeria and the world over in recent years. Gibson (2011) defined entrepreneurship as the process of using private initiatives to transform a business concept into a new venture or to grow and diversify an existing venture and enterprise with high potential. Agbionu (2008) remarked that entrepreneurship involves a process aimed at creating wealth for the purpose of growth, development of the environment, and eradication of unemployment for national sustainability.

The influence of the recent global economic meltdown has left behind a sour economic, political and social impact in developing nations like Nigeria. In the light of these, the government has decided to look inward to her domestic economy in other to build a visible and viable domestic economy that will be relatively immune to the financial and economic strangulations that may occur in the western world again (Ndiomu & Banabo, 2011). It was therefore, no surprise, that the federal government of Nigeria through the National Universities Commission (NUC), introduced entrepreneurship education which is aimed at equipping tertiary students with entrepreneurial skills, attitude and competencies in order to be job creators and not just job hunters. Ndiomu and Banabo (2011) contended that in recent times, the most obvious form of entrepreneurship is that of starting a new business, however in recent years the term has extended to cover such areas as socio-cultural, political and educational forms of entrepreneurial activities.

On the other hand, Shane (2003) described entrepreneurship as the act of being an entrepreneur. The author further contended that, the word entrepreneur is a French word which means "one who undertakes innovation, finance and business acumen in an effort to transform innovations in economic goods. Moreover, the result of entrepreneurship may be a new organisation or a part of revitalizing mature organisation in response to a perceived opportunity (Shane, 2003).

Moy and Luk (2008) examined the career choices intent of Chinese undergraduates in faculties of education and humanities by extending psychologically based model of new venture creation that encompasses students' processes and choices. The model helps to understand the intricacy of entrepreneurial career choice intent in developed as well as developing economies. Their study found that employment creation as well as diversification with entrepreneurial education and alertness was found to moderate the relationship between employment generations, self-efficacy among students offering courses in education. Furthermore, upon their findings, Moy and Luk (2008) reported that, training on improving the responsiveness and alertness to entrepreneurial opportunities will help foster an entrepreneurial culture among graduates.

Alternatively, the studies of Akmaliah and Hisyamuddin (2009) concluded that education undergraduates in Malaysia Universities have positive attitudes towards becoming self employed but little confidence to become entrepreneurs which is reflected by low correlation values between attitudes and self employment intentions. In other words, education undergraduates have a high perception of regarding the attitudes towards self employment or even generating an employment which include high perception of entrepreneurial education, entrepreneurial self efficacy and interest. Interest in entrepreneurship has never been higher than it is at the beginning of the twenty first century (Zimmerer & Scarborough, 2011). A fast growing part of entrepreneurial interest, entrepreneurial education and employment generation have continued to obtain much recognition among social science undergraduates (Bruni, Gheradi & Poggio, 2004; Boyd 2005).

The study of Langowitz and Minniti (2007), shows that female undergraduate students offering courses in social science entrepreneurship intention are significantly lower than that of males despite introducing entrepreneurship as part of the university curriculum. A global entrepreneurship monitor (GEM) that examined entrepreneurship rates in thirty-four (34) countries including Nigeria reveals that, in all these countries, despite the introduction of entrepreneurship as a course of study at the university level, social science undergraduates entrepreneurship rate are significantly lower (Minniti, Arenius & Langowitz, 2004). The reasons for this lower rates of social science undergraduates entrepreneurial involvement, Pearce (1990) contended, is due to the fact that these students' constitute one of the groups most susceptible to rapid employment on leaving school.

Interestingly, the GEM data shows that despite entrepreneurship education in universities of the thirty-four 34 countries studied, social science undergraduate are entrepreneurship rates tend to be higher in poorer countries where students do not have other income options. Thus Reynolds, Bygrave, Autio, Cox and Hay (2003) contended that GEM data which specifies the high rate of students entrepreneurship been more concentric in poorer countries where students do not have other income options, offered explanation between "opportunity and necessity" entrepreneurship. In other words, being given some entrepreneurship education, in the face of stack poverty and no other viable means of income, these students can be more entrepreneurial than men by generating jobs or even diversifying them (Reynolds, Bygrave, Autio, Cox & Hay, 2003). Consequent upon the above, this present study aims at investigating entrepreneurship education and students' employment generation with specific reference to the Niger Delta University, Bayelsa State.

Statement of the Problem

Although there is a dearth of up to date statistical data on the exact rate of unemployment in Nigeria, however local media report indicates that half of the Nigerian population of 148 million are youths, of which 95% are unemployed (Ewumi, Oyennga & Owoyela, 2012). This statistical value in the rate of unemployment among the youths is quite alarming especially when one considers that Nigeria is looked upon by the outside world as the giant of Africa. Moreover, this high rate of unemployment had also been observed to impact negatively on the youths, even among those with university education. Nwachuku & Nwamuo (2010) observed that lack of unemployment among the youths either in the private or public sector of the economy make them venerable to criminality and anti-social behaviours such as kidnapping, rape, armed robbery, and many other social vices which are now a menaced to the society.

The federal government in her bid to address these issues, have therefore made several efforts including the introduction of entrepreneurship education in tertiary institutions across the country, yet many undergraduates consequent upon graduation, still remain unemployed. Consequent upon these issues, the researchers' interest is to investigate entrepreneurship education and its relationship with students' employment generation ability in Niger Delta University of Bayelsa State, Nigeria.

Purpose of the Study

The primary purpose of the study was to examine entrepreneurship education and students' employment generation in Niger Delta University, Bayelsa State. In specific terms, the objectives of the study were;

- To determine the relationship between knowledge on fish farming and employment generation among students in Niger Delta University, Bayelsa State.
- To examine the relationship between knowledge on water filtration and employment generation among students in Niger Delta University, Bayelsa State.

Research Questions

The following research questions are stated to guide the study.

- What is the relationship between knowledge on fish farming and employment generation among students in Niger Delta University, Bayelsa State?
- What is the relationship between knowledge on water filtration and employment generation among students in Niger Delta University, Bayelsa State?

Research Hypotheses

The following null hypotheses were tested;

HO1   There is no significant relationship between knowledge on fish farming and employment generation among students in Niger Delta University of Bayelsa State.

HO2   There is no significant relationship between knowledge on water filtration and employment generation among students in Niger Delta University of Bayelsa State.

Methodology

The research design used in this study was the correlation survey design. This according to Nworgu (1991) is aimed at not necessarily establishing cause–effect relationship between entrepreneurship education and student employment generation in Niger Delta University, Bayelsa State, but to establish appropriate relationship.

Population, Sample and Sampling Technique

The target population for this study was made up of all students that took part in entrepreneurship education from four selected faculties in Niger Delta University, Bayelsa State. The total population was made up of 389 Arts, 382 Education, 241 Science and 231 Social Science students, which give a total population of 1243. A sample size of 310 was used for the study which represent (25 percent) of the total population, which was selected through the proportionate stratified random sampling technique. The sample size of 310 distributed as 97 Arts, 95 Education, 60 Science and 58 Social Science students of Niger Delta University, Bayelsa State. Table 1 shows the sample frame and distribution of sample into four strata.

Table 1:   Sample frame and distribution of sample into four strata

S/N	Categories of strata	Population	Sample
1	Arts	389	97
2	Education	382	95
3	Science	241	60
4	Social science	231	58
5	Total	1243	310

Baridam (2001) defines sample population as the population of the target population, which is accessible to the researcher. It can also be termed as the population from which generalization about the population is made, in view of these, the target and accessible populations are from students of four selected faculties in Niger Delta University of Bayelsa State.

Instrumentation

An "Entrepreneurship Education and Students' Employment Generation Questionnaire" (EESEGQ) was developed. The EESEGQ instrument had two sections, A and B. Section A sought information on demographic data of the respondents, while section B sought information on entrepreneurship education and students employment generation. The section B was further subdivided into three sections. Each subsection seeks information to one entrepreneurship education and employment generation, and contained four and six items respectively. Items 1-4, 5- 8 and 9-14 sought information on fish farming, water filtration and employment generation. All items were measured on 4-point rating scale of: Strongly Agree (SA), Agree (A), Disagree (D) and Strongly Disagree (SD). The face and content validity of the instrument was carried out by two experts, one from department of Teacher Education and the other from measurement and evaluation unit of educational foundations department in Niger Delta University of Bayelsa State. The expert from teacher education carefully reviewed the relevance of the items on the face and content values. The other expert critically analyzed the clarity and appropriateness of each item on the construct value. All their corrections and comments were taken into consideration before the final draft of the instrument was utilized for data collection in the study. Entrepreneurship Education and Students Employment Generation Questionnaire" (EESEGQ) was administered to 20 students that were of similar attributes with the main study in Faculty of Management Sciences who were not part of the main study. The administration of the instrument was carried out twice within an interval of two weeks and the scores obtained were used to establish the stability of the instrument reliability coefficient using Test- retest method with Pearson Product Moment Correlation (PPMC) analysis which yielded 0.81 and this value was considered as an acceptable reliability value for the study. The administration of the instrument was conducted by the researchers. The instrument was personally administered by the investigators to the various categories of respondents and out of the 320 copies of questionnaire distributed 310 copies were found to be correctly filled and were used as the final sample for this study, which represent 97 percent return rate. Mean and standard deviation were used to answer the research questions. For the purpose of interpretation, a total mean and cut-off point mean of 2.50 were used in the study. On the other hand, Pearson Product Moment Correlation Coefficient (PPMC) was used in analyzing the two hypotheses. All hypotheses were tested at 0.05 level of significance.

Results
Research Question 1

What is the relationship between knowledge on fish farming and employment generation among students' in Niger Delta University, Bayelsa State?

Table 2: Summary of mean and standard deviation scores of respondents on the relationship between knowledge on fish farming and employment generation among students'

S/N	Fish Farming	SA (4)	A (3)	D (2)	SD (1)	Total	Mean	SD
1	Knowledge acquired from making different fish traps has generated self employment and capacity building among student in Niger Delta University.	65 (260)	132 (396)	83 (166)	30 (30)	310 (852)	2.77	0.897

2	Knowledge of the use of modern fish basket and nets in fishing has lead to employment generation and increased income for improved standard of living among students in Niger Delta University.	81 (324)	119 (357)	86 (172)	24 (24)	310 (877)	2.83	0.907
3	Knowledge gained about organising fish pond draining has helped in mobilising students to embark on communal labour which is an effort for self employment generation.	51 (204)	141 (423)	89 (178)	29 (29)	310 (834)	2.69	0.856
4	Knowledge gained from entrepreneurship education about fish farming has assisted students to develop of employment generation.	64 (256)	124 (372)	91 (182)	31 (31)	310 (841)	2.71	0.906
	Total Mean	**65 (260)**	**129 (387)**	**87 (174)**	**29 (29)**	**310 (850)**	**2.75**	**0.892**

Cut-off mean = 2.50; N = 310

The data presented in Table 2 indicates that, all the item mean scores of 2.77, 2.83, 2.69 and 2.71, were greater than the cut-off mean score of 2.50. On the whole the total mean score of 2.75 was also greater than the cut-off mean score of 2.50. This implies that there exists a positive relationship between knowledge on fish farming and employment generation among students'. In order to ascertain if this relationship is significant, the mean scores were subjected to the Pearson Product Moment Correlation Coefficient analysis (see Table 5).

Research Question Two

What is the relationship between knowledge on water filtration and employment generation among students' in Niger Delta University, Bayelsa State?

Table 3: Summary of mean and standard deviation scores of respondents on the relationship between knowledge on water filtration and employment generation among students'

S/N	Water Filtration	SA (4)	A (3)	D (2)	SD (1)	Total	Mean	SD
5	Knowledge gained from the use of different methods of water filtration has generated self employment opportunities among students in Niger Delta University.	61 (244)	125 (375)	96 (192)	28 (28)	310 (839)	2.71	0.885
6	Knowledge gained about water filtration has revealed that filtered water is better than ordinary water in the in body system.	63 (252)	137 (411)	88 (176)	22 (22)	310 (861)	2.78	0.851
7	Knowledge gained about carbon and iron exchanger in water filtration has helped students to embark on communal labour as an effort of self employment.	58 (232)	130 (390)	97 (194)	25 (25)	310 (841)	2.71	0.862
8	Knowledge of the use of Maringa seed in water filtration has generated self employment opportunities among students in Niger Delta University.	65 (260)	116 (348)	92 (184)	37 (37)	310 (829)	2.67	0.938
	Total Mean	**62 (248)**	**127 (381)**	**93 (186)**	**28 (28)**	**310 (843)**	**2.72**	**0.884**

Cut-off mean = 2.50; N = 310

The data presented in Table 3 shows that, all the item mean scores of 2.71, 2.78, 2.71 and 2.67 were greater than the cut-off mean score of 2.50. On the whole the grand mean score of 2.72 was also greater than the cut-off mean score of 2.50. This implies that there exists a relationship between knowledge on water filtration and employment generation among students'. In order to ascertain if this relationship is significant, the mean scores were subjected to the Pearson Product Moment Correlation Coefficient analysis (see Table 6).

Research Question Three

What is the level of entrepreneurship education relationship with students' employment generation?

Table 4: Summary of mean and standard deviation scores of respondents on the relationship between entrepreneurship education and students' employment generation

S/N	Entrepreneurship Education	SA (4)	A (3)	D (2)	SD (1)	Total	Mean	SD
9	Skills in entrepreneurship education lead to self employment opportunities.	17 (68)	88 (264)	158 (316)	47 (47)	310 (695)	2.24	0.773
10	Creation of jobs for the jobless is a function of employment generation.	24 (96)	75 (225)	173 (346)	38 (38)	310 (705)	2.27	0.775
11	Employment generation can only be made possible by Government and not private individuals.	12 (48)	92 (276)	174 (348)	32 (32)	310 (704)	2.27	0.695
12	Employment generation is based on individual thoughts to discover new information's leading to economic development.	14 (56)	109 (327)	163 (326)	24 (24)	310 (733)	2.36	0.692
13	Employment is a mobilization of people in carrying out differed self employment programmes to raise our social status.	18 (72)	115 (345)	150 (300)	27 (27)	310 (744)	2.40	0.729
14	Employment generation is the process of an effective utilization of inculcated skills and knowledge in a given societal setting.	18 (72)	90 (270)	140 (280)	62 (62)	310 (684)	2.21	0.826

Total Mean	17 (68)	95 (285)	160 (320)	38 (38)	310 (711)	2.29	0.748

Cut-off mean = 2.50; N = 310

The data presented in Table 4 reveals that, all item mean scores of 2.24, 2.27, 2.27, 2.36, 2.40 and 2.21 were less than the cut-off mean score of 2.50. On the whole the grand mean score of 2.29 was also less than the cut-off mean score of 2.50. This implies that, students' employment generation depends on the relationship with the knowledge of entrepreneurship education.

Testing of Hypotheses
Hypothesis One

There is no significant relationship between knowledge on fish farming and employment generation among students' in Niger Delta University, Bayelsa State.

Table 5: Pearson Product Moment Correlation Coefficient analysis of the relationship between knowledge on fish farming and employment generation among students

Variables	$\sum X$ $\sum Y$	$\sum X^2$ $\sum Y^2$	$\sum XY$	df	r.cal.	r.crit.	Decision at p < 0.05
Fish Farming	3404	38310	46983	308	0.269	0.195	*
Employment Generation	4265	59015					

= Significant at 0.05 alpha level; N= 310

The data presented in Table 5 reveals that, the calculated r-value of 0.269 is greater than the critical r-value of 0.195 at 0.05 alpha level with 308 degrees of freedom. Hence, the null hypothesis, which states that, there is no significant relationship between knowledge on fish farming and employment generation among students', is rejected. The alternative hypothesis which states that, there is a significant relationship between knowledge on fish farming and employment generation among students' is upheld.

Hypothesis Two

There is no significant relationship between knowledge on water filtration and employment generation among students' in Niger Delta University, Bayelsa State.

Table 6: Pearson Product Moment Correlation Coefficient analysis of the relationship between knowledge on water filtration and employment generation among students

Variables	∑X ∑Y	∑X² ∑Y²	∑XY	df	r.cal.	r.crit.	Decision at p < 0.05
Water Filtration	3370	37518	46500	308	0.248	0.195	*
Employment Generation	4265	59015					

= Significant at 0.05 alpha level; N= 310

The data presented in Table 6 indicates that, the calculated r-value of 0.248 is greater than the critical r-value of 0.195 at 0.05 alpha level with 308 degrees of freedom. Hence, the null hypothesis is rejected. This implies that, there is a significant relationship between knowledge on water filtration and employment generation among students'.

Discussion of Findings

The result in Table 5 shows that, there is a significant relationship between knowledge on fish farming and employment generation among students'. The null hypothesis was therefore rejected. This is supported by the finding of the research question one. This simply means that, adequate knowledge of different forms of fish farming contribute to students employment generation in society. From Table 2 it is observed that, the total mean score of 2.75 was greater than the cut-off mean score of 2.50. This implies that there exists a positive relationship between knowledge on fish farming and employment generation among students'. The finding of this study is in agreement with the finding of Akmaliah and Hisyamuddin (2009), who noted that, fish farming does have a significant relationship with employment generation among students'.

As indicated in Table 6 that, there exist a significant relationship between knowledge on water filtration and employment generation among students'. The null hypothesis was therefore rejected. This agrees with the finding of the research question two. It is observed from Table 3 that, the total mean score of 2.72 was greater than the cut-off mean score of 2.50. This implies that there exists a relationship between knowledge on water filtration and employment generation among students'. The finding of this study is in support of the finding of Pearce (1990), who observed that, a good knowledge on water filtration has a significant relationship with students' employment generation.

Conclusions

Based on the findings of this study, it was concluded that knowledge on fish farming has a significant relationship with employment generation among students' in Niger Delta University of Bayelsa State and that knowledge on water filtration has a significant relationship with employment generation among students' in Niger Delta University of Bayelsa State.

Recommendations

Based on the findings of the study and conclusions reached, the following recommendations were put forward.

- Students should acquire more knowledge on fish farming so that their self employment generation opportunities could be created.
- Students should rely strongly on their knowledge in water filtration, because it will help them in their self employment generation opportunities.

References

Agbionu, T. U. (2008). *The Basics of Business Success: An Entrepreneurship Practical Approach*. Lagos: Top line publishers.

Akmaliah, Z. P. & Hisyamuddin, H. (2009). Choice of Self-employment Intentions among Secondary School Students: *Journal of International Social Research*, 2(9): 540-549.

Baridam, D. M. (2001). *Research Method in Administrative Science (3rd ed)*. Port Harcourt: Sherbrooke Associates.

Boyd, R. L. (2005). Race, gender, and survival entrepreneurship in large northern cities during the great depression. *Journal of Socio-Economics*, 3(4):331-339.

Bruni, A., Gheradi, S. & Poggio, B. (2004). Entrepreneur-mentality, Gender and the Study of Women Entrepreneurs. *Journal of Organizational Change Management*, 17(3): 256-68.

Ewumi, A. O., Oyennga, D. & Owoyele, J. W. (2012). Entrepreneurship Education as a Panacea for Youth Unemployment: Implication of Vocational Counselling for Sustainable Development. *Journal of Education and Practice* 3(14): 73-77.

Gibson, A. (2011). *Business Development Service: Core Principles and Future Challenges*. London: Small Enterprise Development.

Langowitz, N. & Minniti, M. (2007). The entrepreneurial propensity of women. *Entrepreneurship Theory and Practice*, 31(3): 341-364.

Minniti, M., Arenius, P., & Langowitz, N. (2004). *Report on Women and Entrepreneurship: Global Entrepreneurship Monitor:* Babsonpark, MA, London: Babson College and London Business School.

Moy, W. H. & luk, W. M. (2008). *A Psychological Based Investigation of Entrepreneurial Career Choice Intents in China*. Honk Kong: Baptist University Press.

Ndiomu, k. & Banabo, E. (2011). Entrepreneurship and Entrepreneurial Education (EE): Strategy for Sustainable Development. *Asian Journal of Business Management* 3(3); 196-202.

Nwachukwu, L. C. & Nwamuo, P. (2010). Entrepreneurship Development for Sustainable livelihood among Youths in Imo State: Implication for counselling. *Conference Proceedings of the Counselling Association of Nigeria (CASSON),* 18-26 January, 2010.

Nworgu, B. G. (1991). *Educational Research, Basic Issues and Methodology*. Ibadan: Wisdom Publishers Limited.

Pearce, D. (1990). Welfare is not for women: Why the war on poverty cannot conquer the feminization of poverty. In I. Gordon, (ed). *Women, the State and Welfare*. Madison, WI: University of Wisconsin press.

Reynolds, P. D., Bygrave, W. D, Antio, E., Cox, L. W., & Hay, M. (2003). *Global Entrepreneurship Monitor (GEM): Executive Report*. London & Kansas: Babson College, London Business School and Ewing Marion Kaufman Foundation.

Shane, D. (2003). *A General Theory of Entrepreneurship: The Individual Opportunity*. Nexus, USA: Edward Elgar publications.

Zimmerer, T. W., & Scarborough, N. M. (2001). *Essentials of Entrepreneurship and Small Business Management*. Upper Saddle River, NJ: Prentice Hall.

INDEX

V

W

ABOUT THE AUTHOR

Dr. Princewill I. Egwuasi, NCE, BAEd, MEd, PhD, is of the University of Uyo, Uyo, Akwa Ibom State, Nigeria. A teacher and an educationist by training, he specializes in educational management and planning with English language as his teaching subject.

Dr. Egwuasi's flair for research has metamorphosed into over thirty publications in reputable and referred journals in Nigeria and overseas. His prowess and mastery of research methodology in education has attracted the admiration of the international communities, hence his appointment into the Board of International Editorial Reviews for three international journals based in Asia, Africa, and America.

A recipient of the prestigious Nigerian Merit Gold Award in Productivity (2011) and Nigerian Hall of Fame Awards (2013), Dr. Princewill I. Egwuasi belongs to several academic professional bodies, some of which include the National Association of Nigerian Teachers (ASSONT), National Association for Research Development (NARD), National Association for Knowledge Review (NAFAK), Curriculum Organization of Nigeria (CON), National Association for Encouraging Qualitative Education in Nigeria (ASSEQEN), World Council for Curriculum and Instruction (WCCI) Nigerian Chapter, and Nigerian Association for Educational Administration and Planning (NAEAP), and currently, he is serving as the chairman in the Nigerian chapter of World Educators Forum.

Dr. Princewill Egwuasi is also the business editor for three highly rated journals in Nigeria, namely African Journal for Education and Information Management (AJEIMA), Library and Information Manager (LIMA), and Global Journal of Academic Research Forum (GLOJACARF).

Dr. Egwuasi is happily married, with two lovely boys.